ILLUMINATING **THE LORD'S PRAYER** IN THE HOLY LAND

WHERE JESUS PRAYED

Danielle Shroyer

Color photographs by Carter Rose

PARACLETE PRESS
BREWSTER, MASSACHUSETTS

2015 First Printing

Where Jesus Prayed: Illuminating The Lord's Prayer in the Holy Land

Copyright © 2015 by Danielle Shroyer

ISBN 978-1-61261-661-2

Unless otherwise indicated, Scripture quotations are taken from the *New Revised Standard Version Bible*, copyright 1989, 1993, Division of Christian Education of the National Council of the Churches of Christ in the United States of America. Used by permission. All rights reserved.

The Paraclete Press name and logo (dove on cross) are trademarks of Paraclete Press, Inc.

Library of Congress Cataloging-in-Publication Data
Shroyer, Danielle, 1976–
    Where Jesus prayed : illuminating the Lord's Prayer in the Holy Land / Danielle Shroyer ; color photographs by Carter Rose.
        pages cm
    Includes bibliographical references.
    ISBN 978-1-61261-661-2
    1. Lord's prayer. 2. Church buildings—Palestine. 3. Christian shrines—Palestine. 4. Christian antiquities—Palestine. I. Title.
    BV230.S427 2015
    263'.0425694—dc23   2015020612

10 9 8 7 6 5 4 3 2 1

Published by Paraclete Press
Brewster, Massachusetts
www.paracletepress.com

Printed in the United States of America

This book is lovingly dedicated to my fellow pilgrims
Joe Clifford, Renee Hoke, Charlie Johnson, Charles Luke,
George Mason, Fran Patterson, Tom Plumbley, Michael Riggs,
Taylor Sandlin, Phil and Stephanie Shepherd, Scott Shirley,
Susan Sytsma-Bratt, and Karl Travis;

And to our beloved tour guides
Nabil Hazboun and Thaer Kaloti.

CONTENTS

INTRODUCTION

've been back from the Holy Land for less than one day. A twenty-seven-hour flight home and I'm seated in front of my computer, heart full, soul rested, inspiration replenished. Two weeks in the Holy Land, two weeks of walking where Jesus walked, traveling the roads of the earliest Christians and millions of Christians hence, two weeks of sojourning alongside other ministers I now count as dear friends. Two weeks of realizing that Jesus is more human, more real, more divine, and more beautiful than I have ever known before, and that there is no way for me to put in words the fullness of feeling his presence there, or anywhere. He is the one in whom we live and move and have our being.

I did not travel to the Holy Land with any intention of writing a book about it. In fact, one of my pilgrimage rules was to be, as much as possible, short on words. In my work as a pastor, words were so much a part of my life: writing sermons week after week, penning prayers, crafting liturgies, sharing thoughts with community members over coffee and dinner. In my life now as a writer and speaker, and as someone who reads theology for fun, I still find every last corner of my life crammed with words— particularly words about God. Much as I am fueled by the flurry of ideas, I also know that the perpetual flow of words keeps one in a continually occupied, noisy state of mind. I hoped the pilgrimage would afford me time to do less talking and more sensing, less thinking about ideas of God and more searching for the presence of God. Of course, my pilgrimage days were in many ways filled with deep conversations about theology and pastoral challenges and parenting difficulties and questions of faith and doubt—on the bus, over the many beautiful tables filled with food, by the fire in the lobby, at a pub in the heart of a bustling night in Jerusalem. I relished every conversation. But on the inside, my hope was to keep my mind open, to keep my head clear, to do far more listening to God than speaking to God. I wanted to *enjoy* God.

● ● ●

On our first full day in Tiberias, we hiked up to the top of the cliffs of Arbel, and we soon spread out, all fifteen of us finding our own rock or perching place to gaze upon the horizon of Galilee and consider the beginning of our pilgrimage. I had so many things I wanted to say to God, so many things I was thinking and pondering and wondering. Instead, I moved myself toward silence, in the hope of quieting my mind and grounding myself in the present. For a while, my prayer was only breath, rhythmic and slow. Then, after a while, it seemed only fitting to pray the Lord's Prayer—nothing more, nothing less. Just Jesus's words of hope for this world and for these his children.

Our Father, who art in heaven. . . .

Later that day when I found myself at the church in Capernaum, gazing into the house thought to have once been inhabited by Simon Peter, I anointed myself with water and found a pew. After a time of silence, again it seemed fitting to pray the Lord's Prayer, and I was struck by the different tones and textures and thoughts that were brought to light in its praying.

. . . Hallowed be thy name. . . .

The prayer felt different here than it did on the cliff at Arbel. Immersed in a sense of place, I noticed the prayer coming to life in ways distinct from what I felt at home, or at church. I decided, rather unconsciously, that I would pray this way in every church in which I found myself over the next two weeks. And so I began a rhythm of entering a sanctuary, anointing myself with holy water, finding a seat and some silence, and praying the words of Jesus, over and over and over again. I could not have known at the beginning what a powerful practice this would be. . . .

• • •

Of course, this is why people of faith have practiced liturgy for thousands of years. In the repetition, we find fullness beyond measure. In allowing the same words to read us again and again, to form us and shape our understanding, we become, we hope, a people of deeper faith, people who can perhaps reflect a glimmer of the multivalence of God, whose song echoes without end.

And so, I write this as a love letter to the Holy Land and to all its pilgrims who travel there (in mind or in body) in hopes of seeing a deeper and truer glimpse of the One in whose steps we seek to follow. I write with the hope that these thoughts and reflections will in some small way enable you to enter into these places with a fuller sense of the unending person of Jesus, whose prayer of instruction to us, I believe, can bring meaning to all our days.

Whether you are reading as a fellow pilgrim to the Holy Land or as one who hopes to glimpse the Holy Land from wherever you are, I pray blessings upon your travels.

WHERE JESUS PRAYED

1

Arbel Cliff
Galilee

• • • • • • • • • • • •

In lower Galilee, about six hundred feet above sea level, loom two towering cliffs: Mount Nitali to the northwest, and Mount Arbel to the southeast. A by-product of the Jordan Rift Valley, the two cliffs stand out prominently in Galilee's terrain. Between the two lies the Valley of Doves, also called the Valley of Pigeons, which has served as a path between lower Galilee and the Sea of Galilee since ancient times. Most certainly, Jesus walked that path frequently while traveling through Galilee.

Psalm 121
A Song of Ascents
I lift up my eyes to the hills—from where will my help come?
My help comes from the LORD, who made heaven and earth.
He will not let your foot be moved;
he who keeps you will not slumber.
He who keeps Israel will neither slumber nor sleep.
The LORD is your keeper;
the LORD is your shade at your right hand.
The sun shall not strike you by day, nor the moon by night.
The LORD will keep you from all evil; he will keep your life.
The LORD will keep your going out and your coming in from this
time on and forevermore.

I lift up my eyes to the hills.

This seems a fitting first official pilgrimage activity. We begin our two weeks with a trip to the cliff at Arbel, first by car, the soaring peak rising above the bus window, then by foot, hiking up the trail to the top, finding a spot among the honey-colored rocks to gaze out onto the terrain below.

Atop Arbel Cliff awaits a truly breathtaking view of Galilee, where Jesus spent so much of his ministry. Because of its sweeping vista, there is hardly a more perfect place to gain perspective and set a tone as you begin a pilgrimage into the land Jesus walked. From here you can see the Plain of Gennesaret, Tabgha, the Mount of Beatitudes, the shores of Capernaum. They are surprisingly close together, a welcome disorientation. Who knew the places in the Gospels were as close together in real life as they are in the Gospels' feathery pages?! How lovely to picture Jesus flitting just from here to over there, traveling from Cana to Magdala through the Valley of the Doves, or walking along the seashore from Bethsaida back home to Capernaum. I never before pictured Jesus like a dancer light on his feet, moving so gracefully and quickly it's difficult to tell precisely when he left or when he arrived. What an enchanting dance floor, this Galilee.

The ancient historian Josephus spoke favorably of the region in his *History of the Jewish Wars* when he said, "Its nature is wonderful as well as its beauty; its soil is so fruitful that all sorts of trees can grow upon it, and the inhabitants accordingly plant all sorts of trees there. . . . One may call this place the ambition of nature, where it forces those plants that are naturally enemies to one another to agree together. It not only nourishes different sorts of autumnal fruit beyond people's expectation, but preserves them a great while."[1]

1. Josephus, *History of the Jewish Wars* 3.10.

"The ambition of nature": a Christian might call this a holy purpose, or highest calling, or the end-goal of creation, this movement toward our enemy in such a way that transforms our enemy into a friend. It's a way of being not only nourished by something beyond you, but preserved, too, as if your very life depends upon it. God indeed has preserved us a great while.

The psalmist attempted to capture this notion in Psalm 121, which is, fittingly, a song of ascent. Our help comes from the Lord, who will not sleep or slumber. The Lord will preserve our coming in and our going out, our ascending up and our traveling down. The Lord will keep our life. The Lord, we realize in our clearest moments, preserves us entirely. We are kept in him and through him and by him.

My friend Susan gathers us around and she reads us the psalm as our eyes indeed look up and out over the landscape of Galilee that stretches out in every direction. Our help comes from the Lord, who made heaven and earth. God preserves us, keeps us, holds us near.

Then we scatter to solitary places of introspection for the better part of the next hour, drinking in the terrain, grounding ourselves as we prepare to embark upon this holy pilgrimage. I set my eyes toward the northeast, looking in the direction of Capernaum. My prayer is wordless and full, a holy breathing, an inhalation of hope and an exhalation of joy.

The goal of pilgrimage-taking is manifold, but central is the practice of being present, of being alive in each now-moment, of attuning one's soul to the fullness of sight and sound, touch and taste and smell. Be here, pilgrimage beckons. Stay right here, in this very moment. Do. Not. Miss. It. In being present to this place, we find holy moments await discovery.

Walking down the cliff, I breathe deeply, and realize something. The air in Galilee feels . . . FULL. Certainly, the air feels refreshingly abundant near sea level, but it feels full in more than just a physical sense, too. It's as if the air has more energy in it, as if it's got more oxygen packed in per molecule, making your heart feel like it can expand in every kind of way.

I wonder if that's because Jesus's imprint is still here, somehow, as if he left behind a trace of his own life-giving force that even two thousand years cannot erase.

I lift my eyes up to the hills. The pilgrimage ascent has begun.

2

The Church of St. Peter's House
Capernaum

● ● ● ● ● ● ● ● ● ● ●

The church in Capernaum that stands atop the home believed to be Simon Peter's is run by the Franciscans, as are most churches in the Holy Land. The church's floor has a beautiful glass opening at its center, and through it you can view the house from above. Its remains are a bit puzzling, as it seems to have experienced a number of iterations throughout the centuries. At first a simple home, it became a known house church in the fourth century according to Egeria, a nun whose travel journals have been preserved and whose name is one of many carved upon the interior walls of the church. Archaeologists believe that in the fifth to the sixth century, the church took on a more octagonal shape as it made room for its many visitors. From the open floor, remains of each of these iterations can still be seen.

The church itself is modern in design, its lines and octagonal shape inviting you into the history of the space rather than detracting from it. Scriptural verses and prayers in Latin adorn the walls, and windows in every direction give the space a sense of openness that seems only fitting for Galilee.

Now when Jesus heard that John had been arrested, he withdrew to Galilee. He left Nazareth and made his home in Capernaum by the sea.

MATTHEW 4:12–13A

———

They went to Capernaum; and when the sabbath came, he entered the synagogue and taught. They were astounded at his teaching, for he taught them as one having authority, and not as the scribes. Just then there was in their synagogue a man with an unclean spirit, and he cried out, "What have you to do with us, Jesus of Nazareth? Have you come to destroy us? I know who you are, the Holy One of God." But Jesus rebuked him, saying, "Be silent, and come out of him!" And the unclean spirit, throwing him into convulsions and crying with a loud voice, came out of him. They were all amazed, and they kept on asking one another, "What is this? A new teaching—with authority! He commands even the unclean spirits, and they obey him." At once his fame began to spread throughout the surrounding region of Galilee.

As soon as they left the synagogue, they entered the house of Simon and Andrew, with James and John. Now Simon's mother-in-law was in bed with a fever, and they told him about her at once. He came and took her by the hand and lifted her up. Then the fever left her, and she began to serve them.

That evening, at sunset, they brought to him all who were sick or possessed with demons. And the whole city was gathered around the door.

MARK 1:21–33

Give us this day.

"Caphernaum: The Hometown of Jesus" boasts the sign on the gate. Jesus made his home here. And it's not difficult to see why. Picturesque location by the sea, serene yet lively, far from the urban centers of power and politics, very near all his neighbors. Very near, indeed. Upon visiting, you get a sense of how small and compact that little city really is, so that it makes perfect sense to imagine when Mark tells us "the whole city was gathered around the door" to bring Jesus the sick. The whole city couldn't have been much more than a hundred people. The first-century remains of Capernaum reveal a village that looks more like a collective, with basalt stone-wall homes abutting one another on either side, and a synagogue right alongside all the rest. They are mere steps from one to another. It's surprising, and less prominent than one would have imagined, but it's no less meaningful. In fact, Capernaum feels something like small, beloved community. Like a rural church where everyone knows your name, and also your business. Jesus chose this to be his home. He was raised in Nazareth, but Capernaum is where he chose to live.

It isn't difficult to imagine Jesus here, but it's a much more human Jesus than many Christians spend their time imagining. The Jesus of Capernaum feels shockingly ordinary, like Tom Sawyer with a fishing pole and a smile. It's just Jesus, walking along the nearby coastline and calling out to some guys here and there, saying, "Hey, leave those nets. Come with me and fish for people instead." I find myself wondering if the disciples thought perhaps they were just going to have an adventure for the day and be finished with this people-fishing excursion by sundown. You know, a day's shenanigans, for kicks. (People fishing?! Whatever could that mean?! Let's go see.) It seems more likely than the idea that they willingly dropped their nets on a whim and handed their lives over on a three-year commitment. Maybe the first requirement of being a disciple is saying yes to adventure.

When they got to the synagogue and Jesus began teaching, the people of Capernaum had their first sure sign that something indeed was different about him. Mark says that "they were astounded at his teaching," and whether "they" is primarily the disciples, or the whole town, the point is they didn't expect him to say what he did. When a man in the synagogue began yelling at Jesus and called him "the Holy One of God," nobody knew quite what to make of it. They asked each other, "What is this?!"

Jesus, of course, didn't bother explaining himself, or even commenting on these events. Even in the midst of miracles, Jesus of Capernaum seems unflashy, as if healing were so integrally part of who he was that of course he spent time doing it here and there. When he learned Peter's mother-in-law was sick, he merely offered his hand and helped her up out of bed. No words or incantations, no mud. He just gave her a hand. Mark's Gospel tells us that the fever then left her, and she got up and began to serve. It seems an odd thing to record after a miracle, doesn't it? He doesn't tell us how she responded, or whether she asked Jesus a question about it, or what anyone else thought. The entire episode was as plain as day: she had a fever, Jesus got rid of it, she moved on. I wonder if the very ordinariness of it, the fact that she just got up and moved right along into normal life as if nothing had happened, was so surprising and noteworthy and different that he had to say it was like that or nobody would have believed it.

The simplicity of Jesus in a town where so many miracles happened is an odd juxtaposition indeed. But it fits, somehow, as you walk around the ruins and glance over to the sea. It's just Jesus, same as he ever was.

No need to make a big fuss; healing just happens around Jesus. Bring your sick to him, just over there at Peter's house. And the whole town crowds around the door, not in a panic, but like people cramming into a house for a party, eager to be part of the action, eager to see all that will happen. And miracles do happen, of course. People bring him their sick and Jesus heals them. Give us this day, we pray, and Jesus gives us the only kind of day he knows: one filled with healing, wholeness, renewal, strength, hope.

I thought of these miracles as I prayed in the chapel above Peter's house. I thought of the people crowded by the door, their hearts filled with expectation as they brought him their loved ones. I also thought about what it might have been like when they all left, when all had been cured, when it was just Peter, Peter's mom, and Jesus, perhaps Andrew and James and John. I imagined Jesus leaning up against a wall, laughing at a joke, chewing on a piece of bread. In those moments, the disciples were becoming Jesus's friends. That, too, is a healing. That, too, is a miracle. Jesus, Son of God, makes us friends. Is there anything more holy than that?

It's just a day with Jesus. And yet, it's a beautiful day. A beautifully ordinary extraordinary day.

Give us this day. Nothing more, nothing less. We will receive it just as the gift it is: this day, to be lived with gratitude. This is the day that the Lord has made; we will rejoice and be glad in it. For in this day, in these moments, we come to know him. Just as Simon Peter and Andrew, James and John came to know Jesus: as a teacher, a leader, and ultimately, as a friend. Jesus will come to be known as the Savior, but for now, as he silences such titles the moment they're spoken, he seems content to be Jesus, from Nazareth, who makes his home in Capernaum by the sea.

Give us this day. This day, warmth upon my face. This day, breeze across the courtyard. This day, in this small seemingly inconsequential fishing village where people gathered around to get to know a remarkable man named Jesus—a man who laughed here, who told stories and sat around talking and eating with friends, who listened and smiled and got sleepy.

Big things happened in Capernaum: calling and teaching and healing. But let's not forget about all the beautiful little things that happened, too. The everyday things, the mundane life-in-a-fishing-village things. These, too, are holy. These, too, when they are given to us, are a gift beyond all measure.

Give us this day, indeed, O Lord, and let us not miss even the smallest miracle.

● ● ● ● ● ● ● ● ● ● ●

Our Father, who art in heaven, hallowed be thy name;
Thy kingdom come, thy will be done on earth as it is in heaven.
Give us this day our daily bread, and forgive us our trespasses,
as we forgive those who trespass against us.
And lead us not into temptation, but deliver us from evil,
For thine is the kingdom, and the power, and the glory,
forever and ever,
Amen.

3

The Church of Multiplication

Tabgha

● ● ● ● ● ● ● ● ● ● ●

Tabgha comes from the Greek word *heptapegon*, describing the "seven springs" that were present in the area. Tabgha, the Arabic transmutation of the word, is the name of the city today. Though some of those seven springs have gone, Tabgha's remote position near the shores of Galilee maintain a narrative resonance with what is remembered here: seven, a biblical number symbolizing wholeness, and springs of water, a source of life. It is a place of fullness even in the midst of its sparse terrain.

Tabgha is a quiet place. That may be because our stellar guide, Nabil, knew to bring us here early enough in the morning to avoid the crowds. But the geography of the place itself is appropriately sparse, giving a feeling of remoteness even as you stand in the middle of the church. The church here, which is managed by Benedictines, was reconstructed to mimic the breezy architecture that likely characterized a basilica that stood here in the fifth century. At the entrance to the courtyard is a baptismal font in a rudimentary cruciform shape that is remarkably well preserved.

The Church of the Multiplication, like all churches in the Holy Land, has a layered history. First built in the fourth century during the time of Constantine, it took on a larger, more Byzantine style in the century to follow, and by the sixth century the now-trademark mosaic depicting a basket of bread and two fish was added. The church was all but destroyed sometime in the seventh century. In 1982 the Benedictines finished their reconstruction, which includes the preservation of not only the central miracle mosaic but some beautiful floor mosaics, as well.

In the apse sits a heavy block altar, under which sits a large stone that is said to be the place where Jesus performed the miracle. Of course, like many of the places, the historicity of the location or the stone is not the primary focus, but rather the tradition of remembrance that has brought countless pilgrims to this place for two thousand years.

As he went ashore, he saw a great crowd; and he had compassion for them, because they were like sheep without a shepherd; and he began to teach them many things. When it grew late, his disciples came to him and said, "This is a deserted place, and the hour is now very late; send them away so that they may go into the surrounding country and villages and buy something for themselves to eat." But he answered them, "You give them something to eat." They said to him, "Are we to go and buy two hundred denarii worth of bread, and give it to them to eat?" And he said to them, "How many loaves have you? Go and see." When they had found out, they said "Five, and two fish." Then he ordered them to get all the people to sit down in groups on the green grass. So they sat down in groups of hundreds and of fifties. Taking the five loaves and the two fish, he looked up to heaven, and blessed and broke the loaves, and gave them to his disciples to set before the people; and he divided the two fish among them all. And all ate and were filled; and they took up twelve baskets full of broken pieces and of the fish.

MARK 6:34–43

Our daily bread.

In a word, the feeling you get when you sit in the quiet of the church at Tabgha is *fullness*. It's not because anything about the church is particularly overstuffed; its sparse environs speak far more of monasticism than excess. But the air, the breeze coming in through the courtyard, that table sitting in the apse calling you to remember a miracle of abundance: it feels like fullness, as when you find yourself in a moment—just one, fleeting little moment—when you realize you do, in fact, have everything you need. In this instant, you are complete and whole and full beyond measure. There is so much oxygen in the room your lungs literally cannot process all of it, but if you could, you might very well be able to fly, or at least hover a few inches above ground.

God knows this isn't always the case. For just as there are many moments when we feel full, we're not unfamiliar with feeling empty, either. Emptiness can fill our days, if that's not some kind of sad irony. We can begin to feel there is nothing coming in, and certainly nothing going out. The desire to be filled, to experience any kind of fullness, becomes quite literally salvation. Our prayers can become fervent, even desperate: Give us this day our daily bread. We literally cannot go on without it.

So here we come into Tabgha with our emptiness, some of it distracting and colloquial, some of it gnawing and fearsome, all of it calling for bread. We get word that Jesus has come ashore, and we run straight for the coastline. People come following after Jesus for loads of reasons, but often we come because we get the sense that he is not empty, that he has the kind of life that bubbles over and washes straight into people, like water seeping into parched cracks along the sidewalk.

So here we all are, gathered around in groups, sheep content to have found our shepherd, but hungry. Jesus takes that almost-emptiness we have, that little something, those few loaves and those couple of fish, and he blesses it. He says, for all intents and purposes, this will do. This is not nothing. It's not emptiness. It's a space where fullness can happen.

Jesus blesses our hollow selves and our meager little offerings and he hands them over, instructing the disciples to go set them before the people. And when they do? It is, by God, enough. It's enough, with leftovers.

When I think of this story, I remember its sister story in Exodus, when the Israelites are traversing the wilderness and they fear that they may run out of bread. Apparently, this is a consistent human preoccupation. So God sends manna every morning, fresh as the dew, and God tells the people to gather up what they need and only what they need, because God will provide the same abundance tomorrow. It's hard to judge them for stuffing their pockets and hedging their bets. If you were traveling like that, wouldn't you stock some away? But of course, their plans for sustenance don't work out as they intend. The manna never lasts until the next morning, and they're stuck having to go out and gather up the new manna again and again.

That's our practice, of course: we wake up and we seek the sustenance of God, and we find enough to get us through our days, but not enough to make us forget Where it came from. For God is a Where as much as a Who, because in God we find our home. Our daily emptiness has become our daily bread.

There are leftovers in this story, too, though we don't hear of anyone trying to take them home. Maybe that's because we understand God's abundance when we see him, knowing somehow deep down that it's not going to run out or go away. Then again, maybe we still forget when we reach the end of the day. Maybe that's why we pray for God to give us daily bread, instead of weekly bread, or monthly bread. God's mercies are new every morning, and maybe we come to get them not because God wants to keep a close, prying eye on us, but because it's good for us to be filled, and to remember Where we go to do it.

At Tabgha, twelve disciples and hundreds of disciples-in-the-making realized that Jesus was their manna. They realized that Jesus was the place Where emptiness became fullness. And every pilgrim who has come to Tabgha since has sought the same thing, hoped for the same miracle. Tabgha, the place where we realize that our emptiness is just fullness waiting to happen.

That's what comes of placing it before this person Jesus. Go see what you've got, he tells us, but he's the answer to his own question. We're with Jesus. And with Jesus, emptiness is just fullness waiting to happen.

Perhaps the better question would have been, "Go see *who* you've got." Or, to put it more truly, "Go see who's got *you*."

That's what you feel, sitting with your feet on the fifth-century floors in Tabgha, eyes closed, air full, heart centered and wide open. This is where we remember that fullness happens. A fullness so full that we almost forget what it's like to feel empty. It's a fullness that, for the moment, creates emptiness-amnesia. It's a fullness that reminds you that Jesus has got you. Each and every day, with leftovers.

And yet . . . what nobody recognizes, what nobody sees—not the crowds that have gathered and eaten their fill or the disciples whose hands and eyes have just partaken of a miracle—is that Jesus is, at this moment, hollowed out with grief. He has lost his cousin in the most gruesome kind of way. The cousin who kicked inside the womb when meeting him, who baptized him in the River Jordan, who not only understood him but started making a way for him, maybe not only out of duty and prophetic authority but also in hopes that it would make Jesus's difficult path just one centimeter less difficult by his efforts. John, who knew who Jesus was and loved him for it, and who was on Jesus's side like a best friend, like family, like blood. John, who in this small and unpredictable world was a face of comfort and a vote of confidence and a walking declaration of faith. John, the one person on earth who could look Jesus in the eye and say, "I've got you." John was gone, just like that, leaving Jesus fiercely alone. Empty.

Here these people stand before Jesus, wanting a world that is full, a savior who can fill them, and here Jesus stands before them, a man who is heartbroken, a savior who knows that redemption comes slowly. Here stands hope, and here stands tragedy. What does he do when he is confronted with this fullness and this emptiness?

He gives thanks, and he breaks bread. He takes this hope, and he takes this grief, and he multiplies. He makes not-enough into more-than-enough. He makes emptiness into fullness. Only the Bread of Life could do such a thing.

When Jesus heard what had happened to John, he returned to Galilee. He stood among the people even as he stood in his own grief and loneliness. He broke some bread, and he gave of himself, even when perhaps he felt there was very little he had to give. What kind of person is this, that he can break and share himself with us so that there is enough, always more than enough? Give us this day our daily bread, O Lord, and remind us always that this bread is your very life, broken for us, always enough. Even, wonder upon wonder, when you yourself feel empty.

● ● ● ● ● ● ● ● ● ● ●

Our Father, who art in heaven, hallowed be thy name;
Thy kingdom come, thy will be done on earth as it is in heaven.
Give us this day our daily bread, and forgive us our trespasses,
as we forgive those who trespass against us.
And lead us not into temptation, but deliver us from evil,
For thine is the kingdom, and the power, and the glory,
forever and ever,
Amen.

4

The Church of the Beatitudes
Tabgha

* * * * * * * * * * * *

Since at least the fourth century, Christian tradition has set the town of Tabgha as the site of the Sermon on the Mount. With its scenic overlook to most of the places in Galilee where Jesus lived, it's understandable why so many Byzantine pilgrims stopped here to eat meals on their travels. It's no surprise, then, that a Byzantine church was eventually erected here.

The grounds, established in 1938 and run by Franciscan sisters, are situated higher than the fourth-century church in order to take advantage of the view. There is also a monastery and a hostel for pilgrims. The Church of the Beatitudes has an octagonal shape, with each of its eight sides reflecting upon one of Jesus's blessings. A balcony wraps around the church and offers a beautiful view of the sea. The walkway leading up to the entrance of the sanctuary boasts mosaics that symbolize Justice, Prudence, Fortitude, Temperance, Faith, Hope, and Charity.

When Jesus saw the crowds, he went up the mountain; and after he sat down, his disciples came to him. Then he began to speak, and taught them, saying:

"Blessed are the poor in spirit, for theirs is the kingdom of heaven.

"Blessed are those who mourn, for they will be comforted.

"Blessed are the meek, for they will inherit the earth.

"Blessed are those who hunger and thirst for righteousness, for they will be filled.

"Blessed are the merciful, for they will receive mercy.

"Blessed are the pure in heart, for they will see God.

"Blessed are the peacemakers, for they will be called children of God.

"Blessed are those who are persecuted for righteousness' sake, for theirs is the kingdom of heaven."

MATTHEW 5:1-12

Thy kingdom come.

The Mount of Beatitudes is surprisingly calm for a place that sees so many people day in and day out. There is room here for groups to stretch out and meet without being surrounded or crammed next to another group. There's room to amble along pathways through the landscaped grounds. Inside the church, you can move from one section to another around the octagonal design, sitting in this pew and that one, so you can ponder one blessing at a time, one after the other, in a way that is truly meditative. The balcony behind the church boasts an alluring view of the water and a vantage point from which one can see much of Galilee. It feels spacious and open and hopeful.

On the other hand, it feels a bit restrictive. "Do not walk on grass" signs pepper the grounds, and that seems awfully ironic on the Mount of Beatitudes. (Wouldn't it make poetic sense to allow groups to sit together on some grass? Can we not spare some money to reseed the grass when necessary?) While walking along the paths, you're invited to write prayers and attach them to the trees, but you have to find a Franciscan sister and ask for permission first. It's a little like being a child in an art classroom with a strict teacher. There's all this stuff you can imagine with, but you're not fully allowed to use it.

I bring this up not to throw stones, but because, upon reflection, these feelings were perhaps exactly right in context upon the Mount of Beatitudes. Spaciousness and cramping. Hope and anxiety. Openness and tension.

The Beatitudes beckon us into a sort of forced stress between what is and what should be. These blessings offer a glimpse into our fullest humanity, the lives intended for us as God's image-bearers and co-creators. It's as if Jesus is telling us, "There will be some people who try to force their own reality onto the world, but blessed are those who choose instead to live into the reality of God in the world, and in you." We hear these blessings, and we want to rest and stretch out in them as if they were hammocks beckoning us on a sunny day. And yet, we know too well that the way of the Beatitudes is not the natural state of things. Our world doesn't bless the poor, doesn't honor the meek, doesn't understand the merciful, doesn't protect the pure in heart, doesn't respect the peacemakers. We are more likely to hand out blessings for ambition and incessant hard work. The truth is, we value privilege, being powerful, winning wars, being what the world would call a success. This has become so common that the phrase "prosperity gospel" actually means something, despite the fact that "prosperity" and "gospel" make for strange theological bedfellows. Does the world honor the same kinds of things the gospel honors? Not yet. We are a long way from a Beatitudes kind of kingdom. We are called to live into God's kingdom, but we aren't naive enough to say it lies within easy reach. Hope and reality are stuck there together, right in the midst of the Sermon itself.

My friend George asked us to consider which Beatitude we noticed most while in the church, or, to put it differently, which Beatitude noticed us. For me, as I moved prayerfully from pew to pew, gazing up at the Latin inscriptions and pondering the passage as well as the Lord's Prayer, it was this one: "Blessed are the peacemakers, for they will be called children of God." Perhaps this is because, to me, peacemakers are ones who can most practically embody the Beatitudes amid the harshest realities of life, and that's not an easy feat. This isn't to say that peacemaking is easy; it is, however, sometimes more obvious when we see it happen. Maybe the peacemakers came most readily to my mind because they are a bridge between our ideal and our reality, living examples of people who straddle the now and the not yet. Blessed are the peacemakers, for they show us that these Beatitudes can make their home in this world with a lot of love and conviction and faith.

Such faith is not without scars, though. We know that too well. The peacemakers quickly become those persecuted for righteousness' sake. They stand in front of tanks of war, and sometimes the tanks fire. They stand against powerful empires, and sometimes they are crucified.

Jesus shared the Beatitudes with us not only to point out what we do not yet have. He said these things to point us toward the deeper reality of things, toward what we can have and do have already in this realm/reign/kingdom of God. And he said them to send us toward that realm with hope and with courage, so that we know he's there with us, and that we will get there, eventually.

Thy kingdom come. For theirs is the kingdom. For thine is the kingdom. These three prayers intertwine in my head, weaving together like a braid, as I walk around the grounds, pondering the intersection of holy hope with earthly expectation. I wonder if there is a reason we begin with the prayer, and then remind ourselves of its reality with a confession, a statement: Thy kingdom come, for thine is the kingdom. Your kingdom come, God, for the kingdom is yours, after all. I wonder if it's because our blessedness begins with a longing for the kingdom, like a prayerful plea. We realize this is the better way, the way that speaks closest to our souls, the way that makes perfect sense when sitting on this mountain and hearing Jesus's words. Of course the poor are blessed! How on earth could it be any other way?! Why would we *want* it any other way? We are able to pray "thy kingdom come" because Jesus has illustrated the reality that lies underneath our lived assumed reality, and it's finally dawned on us which one is the most real, after all. And when we see it, we can't help but long for it. We can almost taste it, this kingdom hiding just under the haze.

Once we have that longing, we are free to confess it. We are free to say, yes, Lord, yours is the kingdom. Indeed we could not see it before but there it is, hidden in plain sight, among the poor and the meek and the peacemakers. It is their kingdom, because in them and revealed through them we see your kingdom. We confess it as God's, and in our confessing, we return it to God. It's your kingdom, after all. We pray for it to come, but we also trust that you will do what you said you would do. Your kingdom will come, on earth as it is in heaven, even if we can't see it just yet.

"Thy kingdom come," we pray, because the Beatitudes point us toward what we strive to have, even though striving for the Beatitudes means resting, trusting, and living into them no matter what the rest of the world might say. That takes courage and a whole lot of patience and faith. It echoes our prayers in the season of Advent when we pray, "Come, Lord Jesus," and we know we mean more than at Christmas. Come! And bring your kingdom with you!

● ● ●

I ended up stepping over the black chain barriers with their "Keep Off Grass" signs, an act I considered akin to holy civil disobedience. I settled into a spot where the sun hit the grass through the trees, lying on my back for a moment to feel the warmth of these words as much as the warmth of the soil beneath me. I closed my eyes and imagined being among those gathered that day; a mother mussing her toddler's hair as he fidgets in her lap, a sheep's bleat in the distance like a shepherd's call to prayer, two little girls darting between clusters of people in a game of chase, a fisherman absentmindedly grazing the blister on his thumb, and the voice of Jesus, sinewy and sonorous, singing out a chorus of unexpected blessing over us all. Blessed are you, blessed are you, blessed are you. How can the melody of God's kingdom sound so voluminous and present, and yet also so far away?

Thy kingdom come, God.

It seems just as far away today as I imagine it did to the people gathered on this Galilean hill two thousand years ago, farmers and fathers and shepherds and sisters all living under the shadow of the Roman Empire. Blessed are the meek and blessed are the peacemakers, though the powerful and the mighty surround you on all sides. Blessed are the merciful, though punishment for disloyalty to Caesar is all you've ever known. Blessed are the pure in heart, though nobody tells you purity comes as much through fire as through innocence. Bless us all as we live in the empire of Rome and wait and pray for the Kingdom of God. As I lay in my patch of prohibited grass, I kept my eyes closed for a few more moments, and breathed. I breathed in "thy kingdom come" and felt my hand over my belly as it filled with air, the fullness of expectation. I breathed out "for thine is the kingdom," exhaling slowly, returning to reality, resting in a trust as sure as the ground beneath me.

Thy kingdom come. Theirs is the kingdom. Thine is the kingdom.

Hope and anxiety. Openness and tension. On the Mount of the Beatitudes we gauge the distance between the kingdom we live in and the kingdom we long for. God, they feel miles apart. What can bridge the distance other than faith, hope, and love, other than mercy, meekness, and peace? How could we possibly venture on if not for our blessedness? It is perhaps the gift of blessedness itself that allows us to speak our fervent prayer, three words of hope and near-pleading: Thy kingdom come.

Blessed is the One we trust is faithful to answer. God bless us indeed as we work and wait.

● ● ● ● ● ● ● ● ● ● ●

Our Father, who art in heaven, hallowed be thy name;
Thy kingdom come, thy will be done on earth as it is in heaven.
Give us this day our daily bread, and forgive us our trespasses,
as we forgive those who trespass against us.
And lead us not into temptation, but deliver us from evil,
For thine is the kingdom, and the power, and the glory,
forever and ever,
Amen.

5

The Church of St. Peter's Primacy
Tabgha

● ● ● ● ● ● ● ● ● ● ●

The Church of the St. Peter's Primacy stands a mere few hundred yards from the church in Tabgha. Here pilgrims remember Jesus appearing to the disciples and feasting with them on the shore. A church was first built here in the fourth century, and the remains of it can be seen along the foundations of the modern edifice erected in 1933. In the ninth century the church was known as "The Place of the Coals" because of the fire upon which was cooked the breakfast Jesus and the disciples shared along the shore. Now it is known as St. Peter's Primacy because it is in this narrative that Jesus asks Peter to feed his sheep, and, taken alongside Jesus's declaration that Peter is the cornerstone on which the church will be built, Catholic Christians consider this to be a clear pronouncement of what has become the line of popes extending from St. Peter to today. By the ninth century a series of heart-shaped stones called the "Twelve Thrones" were noted along the shore, representing the twelve apostles.

The church was built very near the shoreline, and large rocks abut the south and east walls of the structure, giving the impression of being built upon the rocks themselves (with a narrative nod to Peter, perhaps). The inside of the church is simple and understated, its central feature a large rock that lies beneath the communion altar, said to have been the very rock upon which Jesus made breakfast. A sign reading "Mensa Christi" (Table of Christ) leans against the front of the rock facing the pews.

After these things Jesus showed himself again to the disciples by the Sea of Tiberias; and he showed himself in this way. Gathered there together were Simon Peter, Thomas called the Twin, Nathanael of Cana in Galilee, the sons of Zebedee, and two others of his disciples. Simon Peter said to them, "I am going fishing." They said to him, "We will go with you." They went out and got into the boat, but that night they caught nothing.

Just after daybreak, Jesus stood on the beach; but the disciples did not know that it was Jesus. Jesus said to them, "Children, you have no fish, have you?" They answered him, "No." He said to them, "Cast the net to the right side of the boat, and you will find some." So they cast it, and now they were not able to haul it in because there were so many fish. That disciple whom Jesus loved said to Peter, "It is the Lord!" When Simon Peter heard that it was the Lord, he put on some clothes, for he was naked, and jumped into the sea. But the other disciples came in the boat, dragging the net full of fish, for they were not far from the land, only about a hundred yards off.

When they had gone ashore, they saw a charcoal fire there, with fish on it, and bread. Jesus said to them, "Bring some of the fish that you have just caught." So Simon Peter went aboard and hauled the net ashore, full of large fish, a hundred and fifty-three of them; and though there were so many, the net was not torn. Jesus said to them, "Come and have breakfast." Now none of the disciples dared to ask him, "Who are you?" because they knew it was the Lord. Jesus came and took the bread and gave it to them, and did the same with the fish. This was now the third time that Jesus appeared to the disciples after he was raised from the dead.

When they had finished breakfast, Jesus said to Simon Peter, "Simon son of John, do you love me more than these?" He said to him, "Yes, Lord; you know that I love you." Jesus said to him, "Feed my lambs." A second time he said to him, "Simon son of John, do you love me?" He said to him, "Yes, Lord; you know that I love you." Jesus said to him, "Tend my sheep." He said to him the third time, "Simon son of John, do you love me?" Peter felt hurt because he said to him the third time, "Do you love me?" And he said to him, "Lord, you know everything; you know that I love you." Jesus said to him, "Feed my sheep."

JOHN 21:1–17

On earth as it is in heaven.

After all these things happened—after the Triumphal Entry and the trial before Pontius Pilate and the walk to Golgotha and the cross and the resurrection—Jesus showed himself again to the disciples. He'd had enough of Jerusalem to last him a while, so he met them back in Galilee, by the seashore, where he first had met them. After everything that had taken place, here they were again, fishermen. Here they were again, Capernaum's sons. Here they were, eating breakfast, as if nothing had changed.

But of course, everything had changed. The whole world had changed, its future broken open for all to see at Easter, like an egg. How is it that this singular event radically changed the world, while most things in the world remained stubbornly consistent? That's how redemption works, I guess. All at once and slowly, both. There's Easter, and there's breakfast, one after the other, because life changes and life goes on.

So after Easter, here is breakfast, same as it ever was. Friends eating fish by the sea. Jesus knows, though, that because the world has changed, things will now need to be different. Jesus turns to Peter and asks him a question. Actually, Jesus offers him a three-fold question of love to reverse Peter's threefold denial. In other words, Jesus offers redemption. He offers forgiveness. Jesus asks Peter, "Do you love me?" Peter says yes, because redemption frees us and lets us tell the truth even when we don't think we deserve to tell it, even when others might not believe it's the truth anymore at all. And Jesus, eyes full of resurrection promise, looks right at him and says, "Feed my sheep."

In other words, "It's your turn." Up to now, the disciples had relied on Jesus to do the feeding. They had waited for instructions and served as support staff as Jesus walked about the countryside, healing, feeding, and freeing people. But "On earth as it is in heaven" is not just something we leave to God; it is, shockingly enough, something Jesus leaves to us, too.

On the grounds of the church to the right of the sanctuary is a statue of Jesus holding a staff, standing over a kneeling Peter. Both have their hands outstretched: Peter, leaning back and looking up with fingers wide, as if he's reaching for Jesus but tentative at the same time, and Jesus, head tilted slightly upward, his arm directly out front as if he's about to anoint Peter. The sign at the base says, "Feed my sheep." I found this such an odd translation of what transpired on the beach. Jesus was not holding a staff, and he certainly wasn't standing over Peter—or any of them, for that matter. And Peter, though eager to see Jesus and likely eager to find some redemption, didn't seem to be desperate in this way: on his knees, hands outstretched, almost pleading. It made me wonder how we envision authority being given, and authority being received. Can we only imagine it as one person hovering over another? And if so, what do we make of the fact that the Son of God delivered his post-Resurrection instructions to the apostles on the beach that day while sitting around with them eating breakfast?

I wonder if we yet understand the power of human relationship, the force of words spoken with eye contact, trust, and friendship. Is that not what has always transformed us? Whispers of "I love you" from a beloved, a resolute "I believe in you" from a mentor or a peer, even an "I'm disappointed in you" from a teacher or a parent, and always, always a grace-filled "I forgive you"— these cover our wounds with healing salve. We change through relationship and little else. Jesus is Lord, but he did not lord over the disciples. He did not lean over them or hover. He sat with them as friends and he told them how to extend this friendship beyond the shore: feed my sheep.

The Lord's Prayer is primarily a prayer of petition; that is to say, it's a way we ask something of God. Not until sitting in the chapel and on the shore that day did I feel it also to be a prayer of implication; that is to say, it's a way God is asking something of us. Jesus is making eye contact with us and telling us what to do next. In John's Gospel, this is the final chapter, the last story. It is, for John, a great commission. This breakfast of coal fire and fish and friendship is the final scene. We pray, "On earth as it is in heaven," and Jesus says, "Feed my sheep." We petition; Jesus commissions. Perhaps that's the way this new kingdom is to work after all.

Standing at the water's edge, listening to the waves roll in and out, envisioning that conversation where friendship and love take hold after life returns, after all was thought to be lost . . . this is where hope is born again, where new creation emerges. This is where we begin to become who God has created us to be. Do we love him? Yes. And we know now that this love has the power to overturn empires, to disarm violence, to upend death. This kind of love is looking back at us, through Jesus's eyes, as he makes us breakfast and sits with us. With us, because his name is Emmanuel. With us, because the only time he's been raised high above us was on the cross, and only then so that he could be here, again, with us more fully. Do we love him? Yes. If we could, we would spend the whole of our lives on this beach.

But we cannot stay here. He cannot, either. And so he says, "Feed my sheep." Share this love. Breathe this life out so that it envelops others.

This, then, is the message for us at the Church of St. Peter's Primacy: it's our turn. This is the call on the shores of the sea. It is time for "on earth as it is in heaven" to have our devotion and our courage and love. Jesus has shown us how to live, and now it's time for us to follow him by doing what he did. His life was about bringing heaven to earth. Our call is to do the same.

We know we will do this imperfectly. We know we cannot do this without God's help. But we cannot deny or let go for one moment of the awe-full truth that Jesus asks even the most imperfect among us to follow his work by living as he lived, by loving as he loved. Like waves coming in, and waves going out, Jesus speaks: Do you love me? Feed my sheep. Do you love me? Feed my lambs. Do you love me? Feed my sheep.

How like Peter we are, jumping out of the boat to swim toward Jesus, only to misunderstand him, and falsely redirect him, and deny him, and grieve him fiercely once he is gone. Even still, even now, even after all that, we want to be with him. We'd clamber over the edge of that boat all over again. Jesus knows. He knows we love him. He knows, even when he's had to look past all our actions to the contrary. And he says, knowing full well how ill-equipped we are for just about everything, "Feed my sheep."

Jesus leaves the disciples soon after this breakfast because if he had stuck around forever we wouldn't have to start doing what he's asked. We could always sit around and wait for Jesus to fix it. But those days are over, on purpose, because Jesus thinks it's time for us to start walking. He's there still, of course, every step of the way. But it's time for us to get moving.

Along the shore, there are a dozen heart-shaped rocks. Called the Twelve Thrones, they represent the twelve apostles, whose work began in earnest here on this beach. What a beautiful throne, the human heart. From it we find our allegiances, our center, our passion, our identity. And from these twelve thrones, these disciple's hearts, love poured out over conversations at breakfast and along the road and in towns and in chariots.

Love poured out through the sheer beauty of people connecting to each other, looking one another in the eyes, calling one another to a higher purpose and a deeper sense of life.

We pray for God's will to be done on earth as it is in heaven. On earth as it is in heaven.

It is our turn.

● ● ● ● ● ● ● ● ● ● ●

Our Father, who art in heaven, hallowed be thy name;
Thy kingdom come, thy will be done on earth as it is in heaven.
Give us this day our daily bread, and forgive us our trespasses,
as we forgive those who trespass against us.
And lead us not into temptation, but deliver us from evil,
For thine is the kingdom, and the power, and the glory,
forever and ever,
Amen.

6

Caesarea Philippi/Banias

• • • • • • • • • • • •

The city of Banias is located in the far north, at the foot of Mount Hermon in the Golan Heights. Named in honor of Herod the Great's son Philip, who chose it as his capital, it is known in Scripture as Caesarea Philippi. The original name, Paneas, signifies allegiance to the Greek god Pan. Pan, who had the form of a faun, was the god of shepherds and flocks, nature, and hunting, and was a companion to nymphs. Built into the cliff at Banias is a cave grotto dedicated to Pan, as well as a temple to Zeus and many other historical relics. A spring that used to gush forth from the cave is now shallow, but it remains a source that feeds into the Jordan River.

Not surprisingly, Caesarea Philippi was a thoroughly Gentile city, beholden to the Roman Empire far more than to Jerusalem. This northern region is the farthest Jesus traveled, and it is in this vicinity that the Gospel writers place Peter's confession of Christ, the transfiguration, and Jesus's healing of a demon-possessed boy.

Once when Jesus was praying alone, with only the disciples near him, he asked them, "Who do the crowds say that I am?" They answered, "John the Baptist; but others, Elijah; and still others, that one of the ancient prophets has arisen." He said to them, "But who do you say that I am?" Peter answered, "The Messiah of God."

He sternly ordered and commanded them not to tell anyone, saying, "The Son of Man must undergo great suffering, and be rejected by the elders, chief priests, and scribes, and be killed, and on the third day be raised."

LUKE 9:18–22

Hallowed be thy name.

Banias felt palpably and distinctly different from any other place I visited. It felt ancient, like a deep kind of knowing, but also dark and brooding. It felt violent, as if I could still sense the shudders of so many animals sacrificed here, still sense the blood running under my feet. It is the only place in the world I've ever called "pagan." The cave did not feel like any natural cave, such as you might experience at Yellowstone or in the Himalayas; it felt like a cult cave, like a temple grotto, which of course is exactly what it is. This was by far the strangest and eeriest place I prayed the Lord's Prayer. I stuck to my spiritual practice, even though there was of course no church on the premises, no holy water for anointing. Maybe I prayed precisely because I sensed what was missing. The prayer and the place made for an eerie juxtaposition. It was a place of palpably religious *something*, but it was not a place I would call hallowed. It makes sense, then, that "hallowed" was the word in the prayer that struck me most as I traveled around looking at sacrificial altars and pictorial carvings of pagan celebrations.

The story coursing through my mind as I traversed those ruins and prayed the Lord's Prayer was that of Jesus asking the disciples to name him, to give him a title. That has always been a powerful story to me. I can't help thinking of the way God invited Ha-Adam, the first human, to name the creatures around him, and how naming is a form of power, a form of giving credence and legitimacy to someone or something. To think, then, that Jesus prompts the disciples to name him feels appropriately overwhelming. What credence are people giving me? he asks them. What kind of power is being ascribed to me by others? And you? What about you? What name do you give to me?

It seems as if Jesus is prompting the disciples to lay claim to his work. Ascribing a name and title to him will mean real consequences, real risk. And who they claim Jesus to be is going to mean a lot for who they will decide to be in return, not to mention for how they will follow him.

This has never felt more consequential, stark, or all encompassing than it did as I stood in Banias that day. Standing in the middle of the temple of Pan and imagining Jesus's question, it became very clear: this is a real choice, with real danger attached. Here we are, standing in pagan territory, hovering over a place of animal sacrifice and god appeasement, and Jesus is asking us to name him. When we do, he is going to take that name and walk into Jerusalem, upending everything we ever thought it meant. He is going to carry the name "Messiah" and "Savior" and "Son of God," and then he is going to be crucified in a manner that will question everything we ever thought about any god before. He is going to put an end to this place.

Revolutionary seems too small a word.

Maybe the reason Jesus needed to travel so far north, to get out of Galilee for a while and do some thinking, is that he already understood how revolutionary this was going to be. He saw what he was up against: a thousand years of belief in angry gods, of cowering at the whims of the divine in return for favor, of animals dying to prevent your own death or at least delay it.

And that isn't all. He was up against all the assumptions that came in Peter's very words, all the things the disciples thought the Messiah would do that he knew he would not fulfill. All that political power, all that hope of dominance, all that *winning*. This is how Peter went so quickly from confessing Jesus to rebuking him. That moment isn't remembered as a testament to his faith, but it was a sure sign that Peter clearly understood what was at stake here: all the power of the world.

Jesus was going to end this appeasement of the gods, this idea of perpetual sacrifice, this fear of being always on the receiving side of a god's bad mood. He was going to end it, so that he could begin something entirely new.

Lamb of God, who takes away the sins of the world, have mercy on us.

Standing in Banias, in the center of Nemesis Court, staring into the empty grotto and the empty niches carved out of the cliff's walls, you realize, of course, that Jesus made this place a graveyard. He made it a place of ruins, a museum to an old way of being. Nobody worships here any longer. There are no more sacrifices, animal or otherwise. Pagan worship is no longer a normal thing; it is a strange and odd thing, an over and done thing.

I ponder the story of the man at the synagogue in Capernaum, the one Jesus healed. When he saw Jesus, he cried out, "What have you to do with us, Jesus of Nazareth? Have you come to destroy us? I know who you are, the Holy One of God" (Mark 1:24).

And so he did know, more than we did, that Jesus was coming to destroy this way of seeing God, this way of *being* God, so that he could replace it with another. He desires mercy, not sacrifice. This is the Holy One of God, and he is putting an end to sacrifice, and in its place he is opening up the fullness of redemption and resurrection and re-creation.

Hallowed.

Made holy.

Hallowed be thy name.

● ● ● ● ● ● ● ● ● ● ●

Our Father, who art in heaven, hallowed be thy name;
Thy kingdom come, thy will be done on earth as it is in heaven.
Give us this day our daily bread, and forgive us our trespasses,
as we forgive those who trespass against us.
And lead us not into temptation, but deliver us from evil,
For thine is the kingdom, and the power, and the glory,
forever and ever,
Amen.

7
The Sea of Galilee

● ● ● ● ● ● ● ● ● ● ●

Also known as the Sea of Tiberias, the Lake of Gennesaret, and the Lake of Tarichaeae, the Sea of Galilee is the setting for many stories in the Gospels. Measuring seven miles wide and over twelve miles long, the Sea of Galilee is a heart-shaped freshwater lake that served as a natural boundary between a primarily Jewish Galilee and an emphatically Roman Decapolis on the other side. Its deep basin (the lowest freshwater lake on earth at seven hundred feet below sea level) is surrounded by mountains, creating a picturesque view but also a perfect funnel for what can be violent winds from the east and west and from as far away as the Golan Heights. Even as recently as 1992, a storm caused the sea's waves to rise ten feet above the normal water line, crash into Tiberias, and cause considerable damage.

The Jordan River accounts for over three quarters of the lake's water source, the remainder of which comes from rainwater and neighboring springs. Ancient historians mention the plethora of fish in the lake, which, along with the salting process developed in the Hellenistic period, undoubtedly contributed to the expansiveness and viability of the area's booming fishing industry.

In 1986, when a drought lowered the water level significantly, two local fisherman and amateur archaeologists scanned the coastline and discovered the edge of a boat encased in mud. Further exploration revealed that the boat, in nearly complete condition, dated all the way back to the first century. After a seven-year restoration process, the Jesus Boat is now on display in the Yigal Allon Center at Kibbutz Ginosar. Jesus traveled across and along the shores of Galilee many times, likely in a boat none too different from the Jesus Boat.

On that day, when evening had come, he said to them, "Let us go across to the other side." And leaving the crowd behind, they took him with them in the boat, just as he was. Other boats were with him. A great windstorm arose, and the waves beat into the boat, so that the boat was already being swamped. But he was in the stern, asleep on the cushion; and they woke him up and said to him, "Teacher, do you not care that we are perishing?" He woke up and rebuked the wind, and said to the sea, "Peace! Be still!" Then the wind ceased, and there was a dead calm. He said to them, "Why are you afraid? Have you still no faith?" And they were filled with great awe and said to one another, "Who then is this, that even the wind and the sea obey him?"

MARK 4:35–41

Thy name.

Stunningly clear blue skies, glittering aqua water, lush green mountains towering above, a sturdy wooden boat with its white mast flapping joyously in the breeze and its engine whirring rhythmically: there is nothing quite like sailing across the Sea of Galilee. Certainly, anytime I'm on a boat, looking across the water and surrounded by picturesque scenery, my heart is content. But something about this sea, this place, combines all the good vibes of being on a boat with all the energy and joy of being at a fabulous dinner party with people you love. In a word, I felt surrounded—by love, by joy, by the delight of knowing, as Julian of Norwich said, that "all shall be well, and all manner of things shall be well." It was as if the Sea of Galilee had wrapped around me in a liquid embrace.

So much happened on this sea. For one thing, Jesus and his disciples spent a good bit of time traveling across it. It seems as if you can't go more than a chapter or so in Mark's Gospel before Jesus is again getting into a boat, again crossing over to the other side. This was his commute. And what a strange collection of destinations! The northwestern side of the sea was home to the religious Jews of Galilee: Capernaum, Chorazin, Bethsaida, Magdala, Gennesaret. To the northeast sat Gamla, the town Zealots called home, close enough to their religious cousins, but distinct enough to allow them to live as they chose. To the west stood Tiberias, the city named by Herod and frequented by him, where few religious Jews lived. To the east, on the far side, was the Decapolis, a district of about ten cities that were strictly pagan and Hellenistic, vastly different from those of northwestern Galilee.

To Jesus, though, it was terrain connected by a simple boat ride. In Galilee he healed people, and when he made his way to the other side in the Decapolis, he healed people. He was comfortable in each place along the shore in seemingly equal measure. Jesus spent much of his life traversing boundaries. Where others were labeled by place or tribe or religious affiliation, Jesus saw fractured hearts, dismembered dreams, the ache of alienation, hopes faint as a whisper. Galilee's borders may have been separated into quadrants, but Jesus traveled in that boat like a divine sewing needle, stitching up people who had come apart, stitching people together from every regional fabric lining the shores. He was never bothered by boundaries, no matter the kind.

Jesus lived his whole life in the in-between. He lived his whole life *as* the in-between, fusing human and divine like twining spirals of DNA. Jesus did it with such ease, this dual citizenship. We, on the other hand, can hardly remember where to vote. Stuck between Galilee and the Decapolis, we easily lose our way. We get caught off guard when a storm hits, when the wind blows us this way and that. We find ourselves in between, crossing over, in a somewhere that is not-anymore-here but not-yet-over-there, either. And when we do, we worry that we are perishing. We spread our anxiety like a bad disease, and assume that anyone who remains calm must invariably be oblivious to the obvious danger we are facing.

In the Hebrew Scriptures, a sea was often a symbol of chaos, of evil. It was the frightful deep, the Abyss. From it came terrors of every kind, and at its bottom lurked evil spirits. It's no wonder the disciples were fearful when the storm struck. The waves were not just an obvious danger; they were an obvious danger with the added threat of sea monsters below them. The waves beat in the boat so much that it was getting swamped, and they came to Jesus and asked, "Do you not care that we are perishing?" They may as well have said, "Why aren't you anxious like the rest of us?! Are you oblivious, too?"

They had forgotten what Jesus, of course, fully knew, and what the psalmist sang:

In his hand are the depths of the earth;
　　the heights of the mountains are his also.
The sea is his, for he made it,
　　and the dry land, which his hands have formed.
PSALM 95:4–5

They did not yet realize what it meant to be with Jesus, how in his presence we are held fast, even amid the storm, even across the great divides of our lives.

Jesus is not bothered by the storm. He is not frightened by the chaos. The in-betweenness, the unbounded waters, are no cause for concern. Jesus lived his entire life as a crossing over, a crossing through. His entire life, is, in fact, an invitation to come with him as he stitches back together that which has come apart. He invites us to follow him through death to life, through pain to joy, through brokenness to healing, through faltering to grace.

My favorite theologian, Jürgen Moltmann, says that God's name is a wayfaring name, which is one of my favorite things anyone has ever said about God. We are not perishing, not just because Jesus has the power to calm the storm, but also because the name of Jesus is a wayfaring name. We abide in it, and we cross over, cross through.

Our Father, who art in heaven, hallowed be thy name. *Thy name.* Thy name is a wayfaring name. In ancient Hebrew culture, names were chosen carefully to call forth a certain hope or intent. The desire was always for people not only to live up to their name, but *into* their name. The angel Gabriel told Mary to name her child Jesus, because his name means "God saves." And, of course, Jesus lives into every curved corner of that Name: he embodies it, fills it up, holds the whole world inside it. In his Name we are saved; in his Name, we find our way home to God. Thy name is a wayfaring name.

Proverbs 18:10 says the same thing:

> The name of the LORD is a strong tower;
>   the righteous run into it and are safe.

It's an odd thing to say about a name, to run into it as a tower. But his name is not just any name. It is the name above all names, the Name in which all names find their meaning, home, and fullness. "Peace, be still!" Jesus says to the waves, because even they run into his name and find refuge.

About halfway across the sea, we stopped the boat and spent some time reading Scripture, singing, and praying. When we read the Scripture from Mark 4 together, my friend Karl remarked, "I never noticed before that it says 'just as he was.' I've always skipped right over that, but now it seems prescient. 'They took him with them, just as he was.'" As it was, Jesus was already in the boat. He had been preaching from there to the crowds, comfortable as he was upon the abyss. They took him just as he was, which is to say, they took him with them just as they found him as they crossed to the other side.

Just as he was. Fully human, fully divine, fully embodying his Name. Just as he is. That is the only way to take him with us, this Jesus who refuses to give up on either the human or the divine spirals of his DNA. We take him just as he is, maybe simply because that's the way he takes us. His name is a wayfaring name, a strong tower into which we can run, find refuge, even adventure. Peace, be still, Jesus says to us. For in his Name, we will make it to the other side of whatever we're facing. In his name, we will find our way home to God.

● ● ● ● ● ● ● ● ● ● ●

Our Father, who art in heaven, hallowed be thy name;
Thy kingdom come, thy will be done on earth as it is in heaven.
Give us this day our daily bread, and forgive us our trespasses,
as we forgive those who trespass against us.
And lead us not into temptation, but deliver us from evil,
For thine is the kingdom, and the power, and the glory,
forever and ever,
Amen.

8

M a g d a l a

Galilee

●　●　●　●　●　●　●　●　●　●　●　●　●

In the time of Jesus, Magdala was a sizable and wealthy city located on the western shores of the Sea of Galilee, just north of the town of Capernaum. Scholars believe that Magdala is the same city some historians, including Josephus, called Taricheae. A bustling fishing village, Magdala was also renown for its salt trade. Its most famous resident is Mary Magdalene, whose presence surrounding Jesus has sparked not a small amount of intrigue. The city was destroyed in AD 66 after the Roman army defeated Jewish rebels in the region, causing them to flee. They did not return, and soon the city was abandoned, slowly covered over by soil and mud.

Over the years, many archaeologists have attempted to excavate sites thought to be the location of Magdala, with little success. All of that changed in 2009, when the Israel Antiquities Authority was conducting a routine sweep of a plot of land intended for development. While digging a mere twenty inches under the surface, archaeologists discovered a large stone replica of the temple, under a water pipe. As they continued to uncover the site, they found what looked to be remains of a first-century synagogue in remarkably pristine condition. As it turns out, the site had been virtually undisturbed since the first century, spending many years as undeveloped marshland before becoming the site of a hotel. Because the hotel bungalows were built up and not down, the customary sweep by the Israel Antiquities Authority was not required, leaving the remains hidden beneath the surface, only yards from plots of land meticulously and extensively mined for evidence of Magdala.

The current site, which is intended to be a hotel for pilgrims and a place of worship specifically meant to remember the place of women in Jesus's ministry, is, at the time of this writing, still in the process of being built. The church was dedicated in May 2014 and was blessed by Pope Francis, while the hotel, women's center, multimedia center, and crypt/ecumenical chapel are still underway.

The church in Magdala is named Duc in Altum, Latin for "Into the Deep," recalling the story of Jesus calling his disciples to cast their nets and follow him. There are four small chapels, each featuring exquisite and colorful mosaics depicting scenes from Jesus's ministry by the sea. The sanctuary itself calls to mind the inside of a boat, with circular windows aligning the sides and sloping, angled walls. The altar is in the form of a boat, the mast making the form of a cross as it extends to the ceiling. An enormous picture window overlooking the sea stretches out behind it, and shiny blue-green tiles cover the floor and the steps leading up to the boat, giving one the impression of being on the water.

There were also women looking on from a distance; among them were Mary Magdalene, and Mary the mother of James the younger and of Joses, and Salome. These used to follow him and provided for him when he was in Galilee; and there were many other women who had come up with him to Jerusalem.

MARK 15:40–41

Us.

We came to visit the site of Magdala quite by accident. It was not on our itinerary, but we happened to finish early one day and drove past the dusty excavation site, where we could see work in progress. Our guide, Nabil, asked us if we'd like to stop and take a look. Until very recently, there wasn't anything to see. For years, archaeologists had sifted and dug and studied various places thought to be the bustling fishing village, to no avail, until one day a routine sweep of some land intended for development brought about an astonishing find: a large stone, intricately carved with religious symbols, including the earliest discovered depiction of a menorah. Upon further digging, the city of Magdala offered up her secrets one after the other, until an astonishing amount of treasure was unburied: a first-century synagogue (only one of seven found in the country), a wealthy home, three ritual baths, which may have belonged to wealthy homeowners, a public building, and a crypt. All sitting a mere twenty inches below the surface, for two thousand years.

Our group walked over to the temporary site office, where archaeologists take breaks and where interns from all over the world sporting blue shirts give tours to those who stop and inquire.

Our tour guide, a young woman named Maria from El Salvador, led us from one roped-off section to another, describing what they know so far, what they've found, what they're planning next. After she showed us the farm area where a few donkeys roam, she turned and asked furtively, "Would you like to take a peek inside the church? It's under construction, but you can see how far we've come."

A breathtaking sanctuary awaited, even with scaffolding and plastic tarps shielding the view. Truly unique, and befitting the space along the seashore, the church has an expansive atrium with four chapels, two on each side, and a stunning sanctuary straight ahead. The sanctuary, Duc in Altum, is one of the most unique I've ever experienced. Every architectural aspect calls to mind the adventure and invitation of the sea. Even the podium and lectern are situated inside a boat that reaches across the width of the sanctuary, a picture window overlooking Galilee just behind it. Rather than being kitschy, which it very well could have been, it succeeds in telling a powerful story, beckoning us to sit, not in a boat, but in the "water," as Peter was called to do. I thought about Mary Magdalene, and all Christian history has tried to make of her. Prostitute, secret wife, distracting temptation: all lies, of course, none holding up under any biblical scrutiny. I wonder if she knew how far she would be dragged from the shores of truth, how much her deep devotion to Jesus would cause her to endure.

We continued to follow Maria as she guided us again to the front of the atrium, made regal by eight pillars forming a circle echoing the dome high above. Seven of the pillars, she explained, are etched with golden letters, each named for women in the Gospels: Susanna and Joanna; Mary and Martha; Salome; Peter's mother-in-law; *aliae multae*, the many other women who were at the cross (Mark 15:41); and, of course, Mary Magdalene. As she reached the eighth pillar, she turned to face us, making an intentional effort to look at each of the women in our group. "This pillar is unmarked," she explained, "to represent all the women throughout time who have followed Jesus, and all the women who have ministered to his church." She smiled as each of us walk toward the pillar, hands outstretched, almost reticent to touch something so symbolically powerful and beautiful.

This pillar is for *us*, I sighed silently. In that moment, I was given a tangible place in this pilgrimage, a direct, physical way that my own story connects and intersects with the work of Christ, and the ministry of all the women who have come before me, and who will follow. In that moment, I realized how mired in the past I had been while traversing from site to site, recalling our history as the beloved friend it is, but not often stopping to locate myself within it, find my place, or consider the future. But here, hand on pillar, feet standing on dusty, unfinished marble, alongside other women I respect, my own sense of vocation and calling came like a tidal wave, rushing back into my consciousness. It was as if I could feel, gathered beneath my palm, the presence of all the women through the ages, symbolically brought together. This pillar is for us, and for what we choose to do with the lives we have been given.

The Lord's Prayer is a communal prayer, and thus it has the language of family, of togetherness. It has been spoken by the people of God across thousands of years and, perhaps even more impressively, across miles of continents otherwise separated by language, culture, and distance. This prayer is our family crest, our dining table. It is our family name. In our praying, we are knit together, bound to each other, that we may all be one as Christ has hoped. Our Father, give us this day. Forgive us our trespasses. Lead us not into temptation. Deliver us from evil. Us.

I cannot explain to you why, in a place set aside to remember the forgotten "us" that is women in the story of God, the family of God felt so big. I can only venture to say it's because this story feels biggest when it's at its most hospitable, most open, most invitational. The gospel is an ironic upside-down funnel, where making room for the least of these opens the story up to absolutely everyone else.

These women, mostly unnamed, who walked with Jesus and financially supported the work of Jesus and fed Jesus and watched their sons leave their homes to follow Jesus and stood underneath the cross when even his most ardent disciples had deserted him, these women have forged a mighty "us." They have kept this story going, so that we, too, could keep this story going, whispering it to our children at bedtime, praying unceasingly as we gather grain or work in overcrowded factories or sit in wood-paneled conference rooms. These women have broken bread and shared it and spoken up for those with hungry mouths. They have spent hours praying for their families and friends, for the brokenness of a world lacking tenderness and wisdom. They have led churches, preached sermons, visited the sick, counseled the grieved, educated our next generation, spearheaded nonprofits, created stories and artwork and poems and songs of inspiration. They have lived for the beauty of the gospel story. And they have done so even as the church has overlooked, denied, tried to silence, patronized, sidelined, and even abused us. These women, us . . . we are still here. History has not always remembered our names, nor thought to record them. But we have been setting the Table for two thousand years, making room for others to follow Christ.

Jesus has always made room for us, even if the church hasn't always followed suit. We have lived as holy pillars, our arms pressing up at the ceiling and reaching for the heavens, even as we have our feet firmly planted on the ground.

In an unfinished chapel in Magdala, my hand on a dusty marble pillar, I was reminded that the story of God has gotten this far because we have told it, shared it, lived it. And, as the story of God is still unfolding, the next chapter will depend on us. On all of us.

● ● ● ● ● ● ● ● ● ● ●

Our Father, who art in heaven, hallowed be thy name;
Thy kingdom come, thy will be done on earth as it is in heaven.
Give us this day our daily bread, and forgive us our trespasses,
as we forgive those who trespass against us.
And lead us not into temptation, but deliver us from evil,
For thine is the kingdom, and the power, and the glory,
forever and ever,
Amen.

9

The Basilica of the Annunciation

Nazareth

● ● ● ● ● ● ● ● ● ●

The Basilica of the Annunciation in Nazareth is a sprawling complex whose dome can be seen from anywhere nearby. While the Nazareth in Jesus's time was no more than a small farming village, today it is a bustling urban center. It is located on rocky terrain, which is why the house remains that have been discovered often incorporate caves built into the hillside. It is in one such cave that Mary and Joseph are thought to have made their home. The basilica is built on concrete stilts above Nazareth's caves, creating a stacked history of memory that reaches up through the sanctuary all the way to its distinctive gray and white dome.

The church has a main sanctuary, called the upper basilica, which features on its walls Marian art from countries around the world. This global art spills out into the courtyard outside as well, a beautiful display of cultural distinctiveness and unity as each country depicts Mary in their context. The lower level, called the grotto, contains the remains of a church that dates back to Crusader times in the twelfth century, as well as ruins from a Byzantine church and monastery from the fifth century and a possible synagogue from the third or fourth century. But the main feature of the lower level is the grotto itself, which is the cave in which Christian tradition claims the angel Gabriel appeared to Mary. (It should be noted that Greek Orthodox Christian tradition claims the angel visited Mary by a spring, which is where the Church of Saint Gabriel is located.) Visitors stream down the steps and peer into this cave, sealed by an iron gate. There is a space for worship just outside the grotto, too. The dome of the basilica is centered around the grotto, and the upper basilica opens up to the grotto so that it can be seen from above.

In the sixth month the angel Gabriel was sent by God to a town in Galilee called Nazareth, to a virgin engaged to a man whose name was Joseph, of the house of David. The virgin's name was Mary. And he came to her and said, "Greetings, favored one! The Lord is with you." But she was much perplexed by his words and pondered what sort of greeting this might be. The angel said to her, "Do not be afraid, Mary, for you have found favor with God. And now, you will conceive in your womb and bear a son, and you will name him Jesus. He will be great, and will be called the Son of the Most High, and the Lord God will give to him the throne of his ancestor David. He will reign over the house of Jacob for ever, and of his kingdom there will be no end." Mary said to the angel, "How

can this be, since I am a virgin?" The angel said to her,
"The Holy Spirit will come upon you, and the power
of the Most High will overshadow you; therefore the
child to be born will be holy; he will be called Son of
God. And now, your relative Elizabeth in her old age
has also conceived a son; and this is the sixth month
for her who was said to be barren. For nothing will be
impossible with God." Then Mary said, "Here am I,
the servant of the Lord; let it be with me according to
your word." Then the angel departed from her.

LUKE 1:26–38

Thy will be done.

The lower level of the Basilica of the Annunciation can be surprisingly dim despite its ceiling that opens to the vast dome. It isn't an unpleasant kind of dimness, more like a reverent one. Priests often are heard over a microphone shushing people as they shuffle through. It reminded me of a prayer station I once encountered called a womb room, with hazy gauze and sheer fabric everywhere and a quiet hum of white noise in the background. The prayer station meant to remind us that muted places are not inactive ones; on the contrary, even something small and seemingly quiet and dark is buzzing with possibility and activity. A womb is just such a place, and so, too, it seems, is the lower basilica.

As I made my way down the steps to peer into the grotto, I recalled a Sunday school poster showing the angel Gabriel coming to visit Mary at her home. Mary, in her characteristically blue dress, somewhere between a crouch and a hover in this little cave, stared up at a glowing angel who had shown up quite unexpectedly. Her eyes, I remember, were wide open, a blue sea of possibility. I was in awe of her.

I held this vision/version of Mary in my mind as I walked to the grotto, assuming it would be little like the image in my head, put there by a poster so many years ago and embellished by my imagination. To my surprise, it was much closer than I expected. That cave, the sloping corners perfect for hover-crouching, the openness apparent even in the small space: it was all there, right before me, as I peered into the grotto. It was the cave from my mind, with pillars and a communion table added for further decoration. This cave, too, was a womb, its stone walls holding the light of possibility, a muted secret growing quietly. It was open expansiveness in a tiny space, light emanating from a quiet hush.

It seems a fitting place to remember five little words Mary spoke in response to Gabriel in a way that would break the very foundations of the world wide open: let it be to me. We tend only to focus on the first three. Yet, something about "to me" is so important. Generally speaking, we can be all fine and good about letting things be *out there*. To let things be *to me*, literally to my body, is another thing entirely. "Let it be to me" is where the application of "thy will be done" becomes explicitly personal. Not "thy will be done" in that foreign country or that war or with those people over there. Thy will be done in my own body, to my own cultural shame as an unwed pregnant teenager. Thy will be done, that I may not only bear the Christ child and rear the Christ child but also watch as he grows in wisdom and stature so that he exhibits that same God-willingness in his own life, and in his own death.

It is no easy thing to say "thy will be done," as glorious and light as it can feel in the season of Advent. The womb is light with hope but heavy with the price of responsibility.

After visiting the grotto, I ascended the steps to the upper basilica, a much more formal and grand sanctuary with its dome and windows creating a noticeable contrast of light. There is no shushing in the upper basilica. It is more akin to the feeling one gets in St. Patrick's Cathedral in New York City, with people in every direction, clicking cameras and pointing fingers and exploring about. It is not a bad thing, but it feels very different. I took my seat half the distance to the front, praying the Lord's Prayer through again, still with "thy will be done" echoing through my mind. I had no more than closed my eyes before noon bells began to chime above me, and then soon after, the Muslim call to prayer commenced right on top of them. I found myself in the middle of a noise storm, a cacophony of sounds clamoring for my attention, scattering my focus.

The day we visited Nazareth, there happened to be a local runoff election between two candidates, and word on the street was that it was going to be a nail-biter. As we drove to the church, people were lining the streets with political signs and banners, trying to persuade others to vote for their candidate. In Nazareth that day, the combination of two houses of worship chiming and a host of political parties and candidates stumping equaled a significant amount of noise. But it was also one solitary note, pounded over and over again: *my will be done!*

Our wills be done: that is the sound everywhere, of course—a parade of wills. The whole world is clamoring for our attention. Everyone wants their will to be done. This world is just one fever pitch after another of people trying to impose their wills. Listen to me! No, listen to ME! Follow this way! Over here, come over here instead! Buy this! Read that! Look at me!

Determining the direction of our will is an exhausting affair. It is a constant task of prioritizing, clarifying, saying no. We must quiet our hearts long enough to ask ourselves what we want, what we need, when the whole world is barking its own opinions. This is to say nothing of asking the deeper question, which is the question of where our wants and needs intersect with the will of the One who made us. What do we want? What will we do? And is that what the Spirit is calling us toward, in our heart of hearts?

"Thy will be done" is no easy thing in the midst of real life. It is no easy thing even in the quiet of a cave. It requires focus and centeredness and a bit of dogged determination to set your feet toward "thy will be done." But oh, when we do, are we ever disappointed? The greatest gifts in the world and for the world await us at the intersection of our deepest hopes and God's highest will, that womb of possibility where new life awaits. We can pray with all our hearts for God's will to be done, because when it is, the whole world is nourished and made whole. We saw this happen when one young maiden from a cave in Nazareth said yes to a future unlike anything that had come before.

It was a regular day, a bustling day in this now busy city. I was but one of many pilgrim travelers, encountering the basilica for the first time while life buzzed right along outside. I was but one will, and a faltering one at that. What could one person do?! How do you find your way amid competing allegiances and warring factions and this endless parade of wills?

God bless the young girl who said those five amazing words: Let it be to me. God bless her for showing us what it means to live so that God's will may be done even before Jesus taught us to pray for it.

Thy will be done. In my own life, in my own body, to your own ends. Let it be, and let it be *to me*, even.

God bless us as we try to pray those words, and more, to mean them. Thy will be done, O God.

● ● ● ● ● ● ● ● ● ● ●

Our Father, who art in heaven, hallowed be thy name;
Thy kingdom come, thy will be done on earth as it is in heaven.
Give us this day our daily bread, and forgive us our trespasses,
as we forgive those who trespass against us.
And lead us not into temptation, but deliver us from evil,
For thine is the kingdom, and the power, and the glory,
forever and ever,
Amen.

10

The Church of St. Joseph

Nazareth

●   ●   ●   ●   ●   ●   ●   ●   ●   ●   ●

In the same complex as the Basilica of the Annunciation, on the northern side, is the Church of St. Joseph. It, too, is split into two levels. The sanctuary was built in 1914 over the remains of Crusader and Byzantine churches. Below, there is a cave that is said to have been Joseph's workshop, as well as an ancient water pit and some first- or second-century mosaics. Interestingly, the word often translated "carpenter" is *tekton*, which also means stonemason. Due to the prevailing houses and architecture of the time, it seems far more likely that Joseph worked with stone rather than wood. It certainly would have kept him busy. St. Joseph's Church is owned and managed by the Franciscans.

Now the birth of Jesus the Messiah took place in this way. When his mother Mary had been engaged to Joseph, but before they lived together, she was found to be with child from the Holy Spirit. Her husband Joseph, being a righteous man and unwilling to

expose her to public disgrace, planned to dismiss her
quietly. But just when he had resolved to do this, an
angel of the Lord appeared to him in a dream and
said, "Joseph, son of David, do not be afraid to take
Mary as your wife, for the child conceived in her is
from the Holy Spirit. She will bear a son, and you are
to name him Jesus, for he will save his people from
their sins."

MATTHEW 1:18–21

Father.

After the bustling noise level of the Basilica of the Annunciation, the quiet respite in Joseph's chapel can be a welcome one. Romanesque white pillars and regal arches line the space, creating a stunning contrast to the dark wooden beams atop the ceiling. A beautiful portrait of a young Jesus—maybe nine or ten—standing with his mother and father hangs above the altar. I took a seat front and center and couldn't help smiling at the portrait. It isn't often you see Jesus at this age, wide-eyed and barefoot and four feet tall. It isn't often you think of Jesus as a young boy at all, in fact. There is but one scriptural reference to this part of his life; other than his being left behind by his parents in the temple, we have no knowledge of his childhood whatsoever. We certainly don't ponder it, or celebrate it, though we should. I take a moment to breathe in the air, to imagine boy Jesus running with friends outside the caves and down the streets of small-town Nazareth. I imagine him getting caught underfoot while his mother cooks or while his father works with his hands. I think of him splashing water as he bathes, splashing in puddles when it rains, plucking grass on the Nazarene hillside. "Our Father," I began to pray.

It's so easy to forget about Joseph. It is easy to wonder what life was like for Mary, what it must have been like to carry the Christ child in your womb, to make him lunch and teach him to walk and talk. We wonder with fascination and awe what things she must have pondered in her heart. But Joseph goes easily unnoticed. Since he is silent in the story, we can only infer what he was like. We certainly do not hear what it felt like for him to be the earthly father to One who was the Son of God. Did that role displace him completely? Was there any room for Joseph? How did he hold this title "father" in relation to his son Jesus?

I watched as a young family made their way into the sanctuary and took their seats in the pews on my left. After a moment or so, they scooted their son toward the altar for a picture, the mother patting down his auburn-tinted cowlick as he went. He jaunted up jovially and turned toward his parents, beaming. I smiled as I realized the boy was the same age and size, and very near the likeness of the boy Jesus in the portrait. I beheld him with wonder as he finished his pictorial duties and glanced curiously around the rest of the chapel. Can you imagine hugging an elementary school-aged Jesus, all gangly-legged and boisterous energy?

During my trip there, though it was January, it was still the season of Christmastide for Armenian Christians, so nativities and Christmas trees still could be found in a number of places. This was a welcome extension, a refreshing contrast to the "Valentine's Day items up two days after Christmas" hysteria that hurriedly rushes American time. The Nativity was an invitation to slow down and remember the season through which I had just traveled, like a liturgical do-over. The scene itself had the usual cast of characters: Mary and Joseph, baby Jesus in the manger, the Magi, and the animals. I giggled as I saw a cartoonish stuffed figure of St.

Francis tucked next to the Magi, an out-of-scale bearded intruder come to crash the party a thousand years later.

Those Franciscans have a funny sense of humor, but they're right, too. We all want to squeeze in next to the manger and have a look at him. Here we all are, huddled round this child, knowing not what to bring him or what exactly to do with him. What an odd and lovely thing, to behold the Child of God. We are struck dumb, feeling a little silly and a bit out of place as we try to figure out what it means to make room for him.

Joseph had to figure it out too. He had to make sense of that strange dream, make peace with all the strange looks and whispers as he wed an already-pregnant Mary, find room in Bethlehem at the end of a long bout of travel when room was not to be found. "Let every heart prepare him room," we sing, but none of us had to do that as much as Joseph and Mary had to do it, shifting their whole lives and even their address to accommodate the ever-strange and terrifying unfurling of events that accompanied the days following Jesus's birth. Above all, day after day, Joseph had to make heads or tails out of the quite unbelievable fact that he was to parent the Son of God. He was to feed, provide for, guide and teach and apprentice him. He was, one day, to let him go, to watch his bright-eyed boy be ushered up the hill of Golgotha. In all those silent years, in those thousands of moments and little choices, how did Joseph make room? And how did Jesus make room for his earthly father?

And then I heard behind me the boy, the dear wide-eyed, four-foot-tall boisterous boy with the cowlick. He had found something of interest and was thrilled about it. He shrieked giddily, spinning on his toe so fervently that his sneaker squeaked the floor as he ran to his father, calling out "Abba!" and crashing into him with little-boy force. His father smiled as the boy grabbed his father's hand to drag him over to share in his discovery, pointing his finger and talking energetically as he went.

Abba.

Of course.

Abba is what Jesus would have called Joseph, just as Abba is what Jesus taught us to call our Heavenly Father when we pray. Of course there is room for them both. Joseph is no more a silent member of Jesus's childhood family than Mary. Joseph, the one whose hand Jesus reached for when he wanted to share his latest discovery. Joseph, who walked with his family to the synagogue for worship. Joseph, the one who brought Jesus along as he traveled to neighboring towns for a day's work, asking him to pass his tools and hold the stone steady. Jesus needed his abba, needed to know through him just as through his mother what love was like, what trust was meant to be, what faith was all about. He needed his abba. He needed both of them.

Both of them. Together. Heaven and nature, two Abbas. Joy and thanks for them both.

The Son of God as a son: it's beautiful to consider. The father of Jesus as abba: well, that's beautiful to ponder, too.

● ● ● ● ● ● ● ● ● ● ●

Our Father, who art in heaven, hallowed be thy name;
Thy kingdom come, thy will be done on earth as it is in heaven.
Give us this day our daily bread, and forgive us our trespasses,
as we forgive those who trespass against us.
And lead us not into temptation, but deliver us from evil,
For thine is the kingdom, and the power, and the glory,
forever and ever,
Amen.

11

Megiddo

●   ●   ●   ●   ●   ●   ●   ●   ●   ●   ●

Mount Megiddo resides at the western entrance to the Jezreel Valley of lower Galilee. The city was inhabited as early as the Neolithic period and remained inhabited through the fourth century BC. Multilayered remnants of each successive occupation stand as mounds across the city, providing a complex story of military conquest, ancient Near Eastern commerce, and political history. Not surprisingly, then, it is also a well-known and impressive archaeological site boasting twenty-six layers of occupation. Historically stratified remains such as these are known as "tells," so the site today is most commonly referred to as Tel Megiddo. Archaeologists have excavated it since the early 1900s. As recently as 2005, archaeologists digging near what is now a high-security prison discovered the remains of what may be the oldest church in the Holy Land.

Megiddo is located along an ancient trade route connecting Egypt to Mesopotamia known as the Via Maris, or "Way of the Sea." The route dates back to the early Bronze Age. In the time of the Roman Empire, control along the Via Maris was an important military asset. Because Megiddo is situated on high ground at the entrance to the Jezreel Valley along the Via Maris, it could not be more perfectly suited as a strategic military location. With the Iron Valley to one side and the Via Maris to the other, this trade route provided access and control to the two superpowers of the ancient world: Egypt and Mesopotamia.

Tel Megiddo today provides an impressive glimpse into the past. Visitors walk through remains of the Canaanite city gate and continue to the Canaanite palace, which included open courtyards, a treasure room, and opulent features such as colored walls and seashell floors. The Israelite gate comes next, fortified after the city was rebuilt during the time of the Israelite monarchy. Through the gate there are smaller palaces, northern and southern stables, observation points, a public granary, an administrative center, and multiple dwellings.

Megiddo is mentioned several times in Scripture. Joshua and Judges name Megiddo as one of the Canaanite cities they could not conquer, and it was not until 1 Chronicles 7:29 that the town of Megiddo was allotted to the tribe of Manasseh. First Kings tells us that Solomon planned to build at Megiddo, and later we know that Pharaoh Shishak took over the city in his Canaanite conquest. The kings of Judah and Israel fought often over the site, and it is here that Israelite king Jehu killed King Ahaziah of Judah. We also read in 2 Kings 23:28–30 and 2 Chronicles 35:20–24 that King Josiah was killed at Megiddo by Pharaoh Neco II. Most famously, it's where we get the word Armageddon from Revelation 16:16. *Har* means "hill" or "mountain" in Hebrew, and Har-Megiddo in

Greek is Harmagedon, or Armageddon. John's vision of an apocalyptic showdown between good and evil happened here, echoing a similar battle mentioned in Zechariah 12:11.

The sixth angel poured his bowl on the great river Euphrates, and its water was dried up in order to prepare the way for the kings from the east. And I saw three foul spirits like frogs coming from the mouth of the dragon, from the mouth of the beast, and from the mouth of the false prophet. These are demonic spirits, performing signs, who go abroad to the kings of the whole world, to assemble them for battle on the great day of God the Almighty. ("See, I am coming like a thief! Blessed is the one who stays awake and is clothed, not going about naked and exposed to shame.") And they assembled them at the place that in Hebrew is called Harmagedon.

REVELATION 16:12–16

As we forgive those who trespass against us.

For a place that is foretold as the site of the world's last battle between good and evil, Megiddo is more beautiful than one would expect. The views from atop the hill reveal why this location was sought after—and fought over—for so many years. A clear view to the sea, open sight lines in all directions, it's nothing short of a geographical gold mine. It is easy to see why everyone in the region wanted it for their own, scrambled to claim it, killed to conquer it. The layers of ruins stack one above the other like a continuous dog pile of stone, one-upping the layer beneath it in an attempt to stay on top; twenty-six layers of occupation, to be exact.

Twenty-six layers. And that's only the layers still intact. Who knows how many iterations lie beneath the soil, how many times this place of war has changed hands. I wondered if this was the most fought-over spot in human history, and asked. There is no way to know for certain, but Megiddo is the location of the first recorded battle in all of history, and it's foretold to be the last.

This place is like a grim alpha and omega, bookending the violence of human history.

As I wound my way through the ruins, I came to the southern observation point, which showcases a breathtaking panoramic view. From here, soldiers would stand guard and keep a watchful eye for incoming enemies. There is no hope of ambush at Megiddo. It would be like trying to hide in an open field while someone on a hill is looking for you. I wondered what level of force, what size of army, was needed to launch an attack. It had to be a formidable one, for it to have any hope of success at all.

As there was no church on the premises (and for that I was thankful), I prayed the Lord's Prayer here as I looked out in every direction. I could almost hear the approaching beat of hooves and soldiers, the clang of weapons, the shouts of war. *Forgive us our trespasses, as we forgive those who trespass against us.*

That prayer isn't in evidence here in Megiddo. This is a place of conflict, bloodshed, hostility. Our trespasses pile on top of one another, twenty-six layers worth of combat and strife. Forgiveness is nowhere in sight. Regardless of what God has done for us, we have upheld only human domination in this place. Megiddo is a testament not to God's steadfast love, but to our inability to forgive, our unwillingness to yield, our contempt for God's other children. We do not pray here to be like God. We fight here to become god.

The book of Revelation is John of Patmos's letter to seven churches in Asia Minor. In the combination of his visions, scriptural allusions, and apocalyptic symbolism, he writes to encourage Christians to remain faithful to God even in the face of persecution, trusting that God will bring about God's kingdom in the end. It is not a book of prophecy but a book of prophetic speech; that is, it does not tell us what will happen, but forces us to imagine what could happen. Apocalyptic literature uses rich symbolism to elicit a reaction. It is meant to ignite us, awaken us, force us to face the end-result of our actions. In the verses leading up to the battle at Harmagedon in Revelation, John describes seven angels who pour out seven bowls of God's wrath. After the fourth and fifth bowl, the people of earth respond by cursing God and refusing to change. "They did not repent and give God glory," John says. And again, "They did not repent of their deeds." When the sixth bowl is poured, the kings of the earth begin to assemble for battle, gathered by demonic spirits who lead them to Megiddo, ready to do battle even with God. When the seventh bowl is poured, a loud voice booms from the throne of the temple with three words: It is done! These words are followed by flashes of lightning, peals of thunder, hailstones hurtling toward the ground, and an earthquake that separates the city's gathered power. The message could not be more clear: ENOUGH. Enough of this war. Enough of your fighting. It is over. It is done.

Megiddo is the place where God ends war. It is where God's wrath burns against us for our ceaseless fighting, our endless de-struction. Armageddon is not where God fights humanity. It is where God puts an end to humanity's fighting altogether. We have refused to repent. We have rejected reconciliation. We have not held up our side of the prayer: *As we forgive those who trespass against us.* God has forgiven us, and we have stubbornly refused to extend that forgiveness to others. At Armageddon, our defiance ends.

It is done. Or, as Jesus said, it is finished.

At the edge of the lookout point, there is a sign that reads, "May peace prevail upon the earth" in multiple languages. A military observation deck is a bold place to put a prayer for peace.

When John describes the heavens opening up in Revelation 19, he tells of a white horse whose rider is clothed in a robe dipped in blood and is named the Word of God. And let us be clear who spilled his blood, who spilled *all* the blood: we did. We have killed, and fought, and murdered. We have crucified even the Word of God. But he has turned his blood into wine. He has overturned our destruction by his resurrection. He has forgiven us. It is done. It is finished. God has forgiven us our trespasses.

●　●　●　●　●　●　●　●　●　●　●

Our Father, who art in heaven, hallowed be thy name;
Thy kingdom come, thy will be done on earth as it is in heaven.
Give us this day our daily bread, and forgive us our trespasses,
as we forgive those who trespass against us.
And lead us not into temptation, but deliver us from evil,
For thine is the kingdom, and the power, and the glory,
forever and ever,
Amen.

12

Caesarea Maritima

Judea

● ● ● ● ● ● ● ● ● ● ●

This seaport located along the Mediterranean coastline halfway between modern Haifa and Tel Aviv dates back to at least the third century. Located atop the ruins of what was originally known as Strato's Tower, it served as a lighthouse for ships along the Phoenician-Egyptian coastal route as well as an agricultural storehouse and a fortress to protect the inland city and its port. It became a shipbuilding hub in 90 BC during the Hasmonean period.

Herod the Great renamed it Caesarea Maritima, after Augustus Caesar. He spent twelve years expanding it into an impressive Roman center, replete with a fortified city wall and aqueduct, temple and royal palace, racing track, and an amphitheater that is still used today. Every five years, gladiator games and chariot races were hosted there during the height of the city's prominence. Only Jerusalem was larger and more impressive.

After Herod's death, Caesarea Maritima became the primary administrative center under Caesar Augustus. It is for this reason that Pontius Pilate, the prefect (governor) of Judea, made his home here and traveled to Jerusalem only when his position required. The first and only archaeological evidence of Pilate is a stone inscription of his name and title, found here in 1963.

Caesarea Maritima appears often in the book of Acts, as this is where Peter converted Cornelius, and it is the port from which Paul left to travel on his missionary journeys. Paul was also imprisoned here for two years, eventually standing trial before Felix, Festus, and Agrippa before traveling to Rome.

In addition, Caesarea Maritima was extremely important to the early church. Origen, a central early church father, wrote his theological works here and collected an impressive and unparalleled library of Christian writings. Eusebius, the early church historian, also lived here, and it is quite possible the Nicene Creed was written in this city by the sea.

———————————————————

The next day he got up and went with them, and some of the believers from Joppa accompanied him. The following day they came to Caesarea. Cornelius was expecting them and had called together his relatives and close friends. On Peter's arrival Cornelius met him, and falling at his feet, worshiped him. But Peter made him get up, saying, "Stand up; I am only a mortal." And as he talked with him, he went in and found that many had assembled; and he said to them, "You yourselves know that it is unlawful for a Jew to associate with or to visit a Gentile; but God has shown me that I should not call anyone profane or unclean. So when I was sent for, I came without objection."

ACTS 10:23B–29A

Forever.

Caesarea Maritima is gorgeous. Situated along the Mediterranean coast and peppered with restaurants and shops and art galleries, it can feel like any other beach town until you see the stately ruins, their Roman particularity jarring you into another world with surprising clarity. The remains of the Roman aqueducts stand just feet from the coastline, and as you peer through their arches onto the azure sea, you can almost sense yourself peering back in time. With this same coastal view, Paul boarded the ships that would take him across much of the known world, and it was to this port that he would most often return. I wondered if Paul knew what kind of historical domino he was pushing, sending the story of Jesus click-click-clicking along, traveling this way and that as he made his way from port to port on his journeys. Could he have imagined someone like me, sitting here today, a citizen of a country whose birth lay far in the distant future, a woman half-Lebanese, half-WASP, proclaiming this same gospel? Could he have dared to dream such a thing?

When he returned to Caesarea Maritima, this time as a prisoner rather than a traveler, I wonder if he realized that the gospel was already on its way, already spreading, already changing the landscape of world history forever. As he sat in that cell day after day for two long years, could he hear the ocean's never-ending song, swooshing in and out with the tides of the moon, and notice within it an echo of this story that goes on forever? What an odd thing, to be so near a place where the world opens up, and to be so contrastingly confined. I wonder if it ever caused him to close his eyes for just a moment to imagine the cool spray of seawater, or the early-morning fog as he came into port or left the coastline behind, just to glimpse once again the horizon he could not glimpse from his cell. Just to feel that he was still playing a part in the unfolding of God's forever.

As I sat on a rock and listened as the waves came in and out, that's the word I pondered, over and over again, like a pulse: forever. Forever, and ever, and ever. Whether from a jail cell or a boat's starboard or from a rock on the shore two thousand years later, God's forever is often difficult to grasp. But isn't it lovely to ponder? To look out as far as your eye can see, along the horizon stretching to where water meets sky, and think of how a story is so portable it may as well have wings, heading always to an even farther destination. You can almost watch it, this gospel-story-bird, flying toward the horizon, until it becomes nothing more than a dot, a speck, a far-flung hope.

That's the thing about the ocean, isn't it? It's so vast, at least in the way our minds can conceive. We may know intellectually that the sky above us extends endlessly, but there's something about the known quantity of the sea that allows us to ponder the vastness within reasonable human limits. We see the horizon and know the water eventually ends, but we also know it's far beyond the reach of our eyes.

This is not unlike the way we know the gospel story. It, too, is always expanding above us, but sometimes what we need is to see how it's expanding right in front of us, pushing past us, encompassing more than us.

This was, of course, the first hard lesson of the early church: how to respond and adapt to a story that's still growing, expanding, bringing people in. Peter had to be open enough to accept the strange notion that this story included even uncircumcised Gentiles and unclean food. Jesus's disciples would need to see Romans not as a people to shun but as people worth inviting in, finding ways to point out, as Paul did, where their search for an unknown god may find them at the feet of the man called Jesus.

The role of the early church was to learn how to adapt to a story that's always moving, while holding on to what makes it most dear. It is the same two-step the church struggles with today, and I'm not sure we do it any more gracefully. I wonder what we can learn from our brave forebears, who so willingly opened themselves up to a gospel that shifted so much of what lay under their cultural feet. What bravery and trust to embark on this grand gospel adventure.

Here in Caesarea Maritima, where the gospel story literally became a global story, the horizon reminds me of the very tangible reach of God, vast enough to be beyond comprehension, but clear enough to see like a line on the sea's horizon.

The Lord's Prayer ends with this same, open-ended horizon. It does not close, like an oyster shell, hiding the pearl within; rather, it ends with the promise of an ever-resonant new beginning as we pray, *forever, and ever, amen.*

Forever and ever. That's how far this story goes. Isn't it wonderful?

The final verse in all the Gospels echoes the story of God in this same kind of way: "But there are also many other things that Jesus did; if every one of them were written down, I suppose that the world itself could not contain the books that would be written" (John 21:25). The Word goes on forever, speaking anew to each generation. The gospel story is not closed, or finished; it is, like the ocean's horizon, stretching out farther than our eyes can see. There are many other things that Jesus is doing, and all the books in the world cannot contain the stories. They are being written, even now, as you read and as I write. The Word is forever, and ever, and ever.

● ● ● ● ● ● ● ● ● ● ●

Our Father, who art in heaven, hallowed be thy name;
Thy kingdom come, thy will be done on earth as it is in heaven.
Give us this day our daily bread, and forgive us our trespasses,
as we forgive those who trespass against us.
And lead us not into temptation, but deliver us from evil,
For thine is the kingdom, and the power, and the glory,
forever and ever,
Amen.

13

The Mount of Olives

Jerusalem

●   ●   ●   ●   ●   ●   ●   ●   ●   ●   ●

The Mount of Olives is the center of three peaks in the Kidron Valley, just east of Jerusalem. It towers three hundred feet above the city of Jerusalem, making for a stunning view. Named for the many olive trees that grew along its hills (and still do), it is referenced often in both the Old and New Testaments. King David came here to weep when he learned of Absalom's conniving plans to overtake the throne (2 Samuel 15). When Ezekiel had a vision of the glory of the Lord leaving the temple, that glory stopped on the Mount of Olives (Ezekiel 11). Zechariah prophesied that the Mount of Olives would be the place where the Lord would stand and judge the people, so that the mountain would be split in two (Zechariah 14). Because of this prophecy, the mount has long been a Jewish burial site.

The Mount of Olives is on a well-traveled path from Jerusalem to Bethany, one Jesus would have traveled frequently. Luke's Gospel tells us that Jesus spent the night on the Mount of Olives often (Luke 21), and this included the night of his betrayal (Luke 22). It is on the Mount of Olives that Jesus wept for Jerusalem during his triumphal entry (Luke 19).

The church that sits on the mount today is Dominus Flevit. Translated "The Lord Wept," it is designed in the shape of a teardrop and has an appropriately sparse interior. Tear phials perch solemnly at the four corners of the dome, and a mosaic beneath the altar depicts a hen gathering chicks under her wings. The church was built in 1955, but it rests upon the remains of a Byzantine one that had been dedicated to the prophet Anna. A large arched picture window faces west toward Jerusalem and has a symbol of a chalice and a cross, between which one can see the Church of the Holy Sepulchre, the traditional place of Golgotha and the empty tomb.

When he had come near Bethphage and Bethany, at the place called the Mount of Olives, he sent two of the disciples, saying, "Go into the village ahead of you, and as you enter it you will find tied there a colt that has never been ridden. Untie it and bring it here. . . ."

As he came near and saw the city, he wept over it, saying, "If you, even you, had only recognized on this day the things that make for peace!"

LUKE 19:29–30, 41–42A

The layered ruins of Megiddo

The Sea of Galilee

The Church of All Nations, Gethsemane

Chapel of the Angels, Shepherds Field, Bethlehem

Bethesda

Via Dolorosa, Jerusalem

Via Dolorosa amid the bustling Jerusalem Cardo

Church of the Holy Sepulchre, Jerusalem

The Valley of the Doves near the cliffs of Arbel,
where Jesus likely walked while in Galilee

The view from the Mount of the Beatitudes over Galilee

Who art in heaven.

Dominus Flevit is a place for weeping. Here on the mount, over-looking the sweeping panoramic view of Jerusalem, it is easy to remember Jesus's tears. He came near to this place, and he, too, looked out onto the city. In the distance stood the Praetorium, Herod's sprawling palace, stretching a thousand feet from north to south. Beside it were Herod's three fortified towers, rising over a hundred feet in the air. Below was the heart of the city, people traveling across streets, houses peppering the landscape. Straight ahead stood the temple, majestic with its marbled porticoes and bronze doors. The city of Jerusalem teemed with energy and life, displayed only moments earlier in a rousing triumphal parade that greeted Jesus on its outskirts as he walked toward the mount on his way into the city. But what Jesus saw that day, despite the cloaks spread at his feet or the palms being waved up and down or the shouts of "Hosanna!" by the crowd that had gathered, was a city that was divided, divisive, and headed for war.

In two thousand years, the view has changed somewhat. The temple, the Praetorium, and the towers are gone, and other prom-inent buildings have taken their place. If Jesus were to stand on the Mount of Olives today, his eyes would see a city divided and divisive.

God help us if we do not weep over Jerusalem still.

So much of this pilgrimage has been a reminder of the nearness, fullness, and closeness of God. The Mount of Olives is the place where you weep over our distance from God. Our Father, who art in heaven, and who seems so very, very far away from the warring hearts of his children. Our Father, who art in heaven, who wants to gather us together while we seem hell-bent on scattering apart. Our Father, who art in heaven, who sees the infighting and the violence and the hatred and the bloodshed for exactly what it is:

a far cry from the reign of God where lion and lamb lie peaceably together, where we are all made whole, and one.

Heaven seemed a million miles away.

As I made my way into Dominus Flevit, the tears already brimming at my eyes like a fountain of broken promises, I sat down heavily, with a thud, and stared through the window to the cityscape ahead, praying the Lord's Prayer once, twice, a third and fourth time, all the while spiraling down into the deep reality of our broken civilizations. It struck me so deeply, this crux of tension between what is and what ought to be, between Golgotha and Easter, between a broken and divided Jerusalem and a whole and healed kingdom. It was as if I could feel the heaviness of the place and all the burdens it carries, as if the heaviness of Jesus's sadness became almost excruciatingly palpable. In the same way that Moses could not experience the fullness of God's glory, Dominus Flevit reminds us that we cannot experience the fullness of God's pain. To see his children at war, for so long, to such sorrowful ends: do we even know how to begin to understand how that breaks the heart of God? How that ripples defiantly through heaven like a misplaced battle cry against our very selves, our own best interests, our deepest purposes? What do we do with this deep knowledge that Jesus would do *anything* to bridge the two, to bring them together, to convince us to give up our destructive ways and seek life? What do we do with the knowledge that he would be torn and bloodied for its division, raised for its salvation, and still find a Jerusalem at war two thousand years later?

We weep.

Our Father, who art in heaven, who so loved the world that you gave your only begotten Son so that everyone who believes in you will not perish: we are perishing still, your people. We are not only perishing, but killing. We are erecting walls, manning checkpoints, throwing bombs, delivering sanctions, murdering the innocent, squeezing pocketbooks, throwing stones. We do not know the things that make for peace. We do not recognize them. And if we recognize them, we do not choose them. Not even in this holy city.

If you could not teach us, Jesus, if we could not listen even to you, what hope do we have of knowing the ways of peace?

Under the tear-shaped dome of Dominus Flevit Church, one can become undone. In that place, as you stare at the window ahead, etched with a chalice and a cross, the pain of the Lord passes by like a harrowing cloud, and there is no rock to shield you from it. All the fighting, up to the present day, over this place, can sweep over you like a tidal wave, reminding you of the pervasive pain of suffering and violence and discord that runs rampant through this world. Dominus Flevit is a necessary reminder of why God's Spirit still comes to comfort us, still must sustain us, lest we die.

In this place, Jesus did not feel like friend or companion or teacher. Here, in the echoing shadow of his words, Jesus was clearly and unequivocally GOD, standing in stark contrast to all we've misunderstood, all we've yet to see, all we've yet to do. Jesus, who lived his humanity with goodness and grace, can only weep at his children who seem so bent on their own destruction. Our Father, who art in heaven, we cannot do this alone. We cannot be counted upon to know or to do those things that make for peace. Send your Spirit to comfort us in our woundedness. Send your Son to gather us under his wings as a mother hen gathers her chicks. We know we are broken. We know we are scattered. We know we are far from you. Weep for us out of your deep love and your everlasting faithfulness, and bring us home.

● ● ● ● ● ● ● ● ● ● ●

Our Father, who art in heaven, hallowed be thy name;
Thy kingdom come, thy will be done on earth as it is in heaven.
Give us this day our daily bread, and forgive us our trespasses,
as we forgive those who trespass against us.
And lead us not into temptation, but deliver us from evil,
For thine is the kingdom, and the power, and the glory,
forever and ever,
Amen.

14

The Church of All Nations
Gethsemane/Jerusalem

● ● ● ● ● ● ● ● ● ● ●

Gethsemane, which means "oil press," resides at the foot of the Mount of Olives and faces Jerusalem (and the Temple Mount, specifically). The olive grove here has been well preserved with a garden that is home to trees thousands of years old. We know that Jesus came to this garden of olive trees on the evening of the Passover Feast, after the Last Supper, and it was here that he prayed, was betrayed, arrested.

On this site today is the Church of All Nations, also known as the Church of Agony. It was named the Church of All Nations to honor the many nations who raised funds to have its basilica built in the 1920s. An understated coat-of-arms in honor of each of these nations peppers the domed ceilings. A Byzantine (fourth-century) church stood here previously, but it was destroyed during an earthquake in 746. A Crusader church took its place in the twelfth century, but by 1187 it too was destroyed.

At the front of the church is a large stone called the Rock of Agony, said to have been the stone upon which Jesus wept. Around its perimeter there is a short iron gate that features a crown of thorns and olive branches intertwined, as well as two birds flanking a chalice, a symbol of those who willingly follow in the footsteps of the crucified Christ.

They went to a place called Gethsemane; and he said to his disciples, "Sit here while I pray." He took with him Peter and James and John, and began to be distressed and agitated. And he said to them, "I am deeply grieved, even to death; remain here, and keep awake." And going a little farther, he threw himself on the ground and prayed that, if it were possible, the hour might pass from him. He said, "Abba, Father, for you all things are possible; remove this cup from me; yet, not what I want, but what you want." He came and found them sleeping; and he said to Peter, "Simon, are you asleep? Could you not keep awake one hour? Keep awake and pray that you may not come into the time of trial; the spirit indeed is willing, but the flesh is weak." And again he went away and prayed, saying the same words. And once more he came and found them sleeping, for their eyes were very heavy; and they did not know what to say to him. He came a third time and said to them, "Are you still sleeping and taking your rest? Enough! The hour has come; the Son of Man is betrayed into the hands of sinners. Get up, let us be going. See, my betrayer is at hand."

Mark 14:32–42

Lead us not into temptation.

The first thing you notice when you walk into the Church of Agony is the deep, melancholy color of the place. The stained-glass windows along each side are made from purple alabaster, through which very little light comes through. Each window is composed of geometric squares, five of which make up a cross. The ceiling, covered in deep blue, was intentionally kept low through the use of multiple small domes to convey a sense of heaviness and depression. Exquisitely detailed mosaics depicting scenes from the night of Jesus's betrayal reside along the walls and in corners. The Church of Agony is an agonizingly beautiful place.

I made my way to the front of the church, where the Rock of Agony resides in front of the altar, and knelt to pray. The white marble slab upon which my arms rested was shockingly cold, almost to the point of distraction. I prayed the Lord's Prayer a number of times, each time the phrase "lead us not into temptation" catching in my throat, a lump of regret for all the ways all of us have left Jesus when he needed us, chosen our own safety or comfort over righteousness, fallen asleep in the middle of a world that is asking for our attention. Could we not keep awake?

Amid the shuffle of feet and digital photograph clicks, there is still a known silence here. A Franciscan priest reminds us often over a microphone of our job in this place: "Silence, please. Silencio." I can't imagine anyone wanting to do otherwise. This is not the place for talk, and God knows it's not the place for sleep, either. Gethsemane is where we sit in solidarity with the One who will suffer the weight of the world. We cannot fix it for him. We cannot take the cup from him. The only thing we can do, the only thing he asks of us, is to keep watch with him as he readies himself for what is next. What the deep alabaster recalls to me most painfully is not that Jesus suffered, but that before Jesus suffered, he asked his friends to sit with him, and they fell asleep on him instead. In his greatest hour of need, in the most vulnerable space a human can occupy, he needed not saviors, not fixers, but friends. And, God help us, we fell asleep instead.

What those purple walls said to me, what that blue ceiling echoed, was that Jesus was painfully and irrevocably alone that night. I wish I could fix that for him, but I know of course that I would have fallen asleep on him, too. Or worse, I would have stayed up, and tried to convince him to flee to Bethany, or tried to give him a pep talk about how it was all going to work out in the end. How I wish to God we could learn the deep mystery of what it means to be asked simply to hold his hand in his hour of despair, to grasp the trembling palm of this Emmanuel, God-with-us, so that he knew in some small way that we also desperately want to be us-with-God.

Could we not stay with him but one hour? Could we not sit still and be present to this moment?

I was jarred out of my thoughts by a group of pilgrims who began to sing at the Rock of Agony. They were singing the simple chorus of Alleluia, that one word over and over and over again. It was beautiful to hear their melodies echo, to imagine that word of praise in a new way through the lens of Gethsemane's agony. It sounded like thankfulness for Jesus's faithfulness, particularly despite our own lack. The priest did not shush them. And yet when the song was over, and when I left the sanctuary and walked the length of the garden, my friend Michael mentioned his frustration over this act. First, it is a place of silence, not of singing, and that ought to be respected. Second, it's not the place for alleluias.

He is right. There is something deeply important about holding space here only for sorrow. This is the one church in the entire world where singing isn't encouraged, and there's a very good reason for it, one that forms us deeply if we adhere to it. In this church, we are asked to sit with Jesus's suffering and set down all the ways we try to avoid it, including our own praise of him. What does it mean that even in this agonizing place we feel compelled to bring our alleluias? Could we not wait with him one hour?

Lead us not into temptation. Even in the way we often pray this, we think only of ourselves. What comes to mind is our most pressing personal struggle, rather than our propensity to avoid seeing the struggles of others. We ponder how we can maintain our own righteousness and not how our actions have imposed upon the righteousness of others. There is a danger in seeing temptation as something so me-centered, so private and small. And not only that, we then rush headlong toward the finish line of redemption, no matter where we happen to be located on the track. We forget that, as freely and fully as redemption is offered us, it's not always instantaneous in the way we live it out in this flesh-and-blood world. Even grace cannot undo what has been done. It can only give us a way forward. It can only promise a better future, not undo the pain of the past, or even the necessary difficulty of the present. Sometimes, our faith calls us to sit and wait, to let the finish line loom ahead of us. This can be so painful. It can almost undo us. But so can our attempts to make God into our own image.

It is a temptation to rush toward Easter and minimize much of what made Easter possible and necessary. One of those holy redemption moments is the fact that at the Garden of Gethsemane what Jesus needed most was the solidarity of his friends, and they fell asleep on him instead. And when they were not falling asleep, they were rebuking his pronouncements or misunderstanding his mission or imagining their own places of power and honor. They were eager to sing their alleluias when it was not yet time. We could not wait with him. We could not accept what was going to happen. We could not take his hand, sit next to him, and be present.

All of us have left Jesus when he needed us, chosen our own safety or comfort over righteousness, fallen asleep in the middle of a world that is asking for our attention. Could we not keep awake? Could we not be still, sit beside sadness, dwell with grief, even await unavoidable suffering? Are we so eager to grab onto our victories that we trample over the suffering Christ to reach them? Are we longing so urgently for resurrection that we abandon our Lord on the way, leaving him alone in the garden? Is our denial of suffering so strong, so pervasive, that we have forgotten we follow a crucified God?

Lead us not into temptation, Lord. Keep us steady and present. Hush our alleluias when our silence is needed more.

● ● ● ● ● ● ● ● ● ● ●

Our Father, who art in heaven, hallowed be thy name;
Thy kingdom come, thy will be done on earth as it is in heaven.
Give us this day our daily bread, and forgive us our trespasses,
as we forgive those who trespass against us.
And lead us not into temptation, but deliver us from evil,
For thine is the kingdom, and the power, and the glory,
forever and ever,
Amen.

15

The Church of St. Peter in Gallicantu

Jerusalem

●   ●   ●   ●   ●   ●   ●   ●   ●   ●   ●

On the eastern hillside of Mount Zion stands the Church of St. Peter in Gallicantu. Built in 1932 by the French religious order the Assumptionists, the church is said to be the place where Peter denied Jesus on the night of his arrest. The courtyard of Gallicantu, which means "cock crow" in Latin, features a harrowing statue of Peter, the woman who questioned him, and a Roman soldier providing a somber place to contemplate this event.

It is also potentially the location of Caiaphas's house, where Jesus was jailed the night before his trial and crucifixion. Archaeologists remain split over the location of Caiaphas's house, but early Christians marked one of the prisoner's cells here with a cross, presumably because this is the one believed to have held Jesus overnight. To be specific, what is marked is a hole from above, through which a prisoner would be dropped ten feet to the cell below by a rope. Both the hole and the prison cell are accessible within the church.

As per usual, the church is built upon the remains of previous churches from the Byzantine and Crusader eras. Originally built in 457, it was rebuilt in 628 and then again in 1100. Two of the Byzantine-era mosaics survive, and they can be seen to the right as you enter. The church has four levels, including a sanctuary, chapel, dungeon, and what is called the Sacred Pit or Jesus's Prison. The dungeon and pit are below, with the chapel perched in the middle and the sanctuary up top. The chapel is muted, with white arched ceilings and three mosaics fanning out as three altars across the front. One outside wall features colorful stained glass, which is echoed above as well. The sanctuary is far grander, featuring a number of moving narrative mosaics and a spectacular cross-shaped window in the domed ceiling.

Outside the church, there is a paved path of stones that archaeologists agree dates back to the time of Jesus. Most agree it was along this route that Jesus was taken that night, regardless of whether this is the house where he was brought. In fact, this is a path Jesus certainly took on many occasions.

Now Peter was sitting outside in the courtyard. A servant-girl came to him and said, "You also were with Jesus the Galilean." But he denied it before all of them, saying, "I do not know what you are talking about." When he went out to the porch, another servant-girl saw him, and she said to the bystanders, "This man was with Jesus of Nazareth." Again he denied it with an oath, "I do not know the man." After a little while

the bystanders came up and said to Peter, "Certainly
you are also one of them, for your accent betrays you."
Then he began to curse, and he swore an oath, "I do
not know the man!" At that moment the cock crowed.
Then Peter remembered what Jesus had said: "Before
the cock crows, you will deny me three times." And he
went out and wept bitterly.

MATTHEW 26:69–75

Forgive us our trespasses.

I can't say that I have ever heard of a church whose entire existence
and very name is meant to recall one person's worst mistake. There
is no Church of the Nine Healed Lepers Who Never Said Thank
You. There is no Church of the Thirty Silver Pieces. There's not
a Church of the Extramarital Affair or Church of the Embezzled
Tithes. So for a church to be named for Peter's biggest mistake
seems odd at best and shameful at worst. If our worst mistake just
happened to be committed in conjunction with one of the biggest
events in all of history, I doubt we would want it remembered at
all, much less with a building.

As we made our way toward the church, I noticed a golden
rooster perched atop the central blue dome. There was a cross atop
another, smaller dome, but the rooster was central. As we rounded
a corner, I saw a mosaic square depicting a rooster on the wall, with
an arrow beneath it, presumably pointing us in the proper direction
of the church. When we reached the large double doors, they were
etched with a scene of Jesus predicting Peter's death.

This church was not merely named for Peter's mistake: it practically
enshrined it.

Before we entered, we took a few moments in the courtyard. Whatever witty sarcasm I may have had about the church came to a screeching halt as I surveyed the bronze statue of Peter, two servant girls, and a Roman soldier. At its base are the Latin words *Non Novi Illum*: "I do not know him." Peter's hands are up, cast to the side as if to cast off any such false accusation like an old coat. He doesn't have time for this nonsense, he says in his body language. He does not know this man. He doesn't even know what they are talking about.

Staring at that statue is like facing your worst fear. It's hard not to wonder what you would have done, whether you would have claimed him, if it had been you in that courtyard. We all would like to think we would choose differently; I'm not at all certain that's true. Gazing at the frozen Roman soldier, imagining the events of that night, of the arrest in the garden, of the swirling accusations and the heightened rumors, of the very dark sense that whatever this was, was over . . . who among us would easily claim our Christ without hesitation?

I do not know where the other disciples went after Jesus was arrested. Maybe they went home, and maybe they hid in the busy streets of the city. Maybe they were only around the corner, far enough away to prevent the accusations that fell so heavily on Peter's shoulders. But Peter was here. Jesus was inside, being held in a small, cold cell. And Peter, for whatever it's worth, stayed near him.

And then he denied him, three times.

Non novi illum. I do not know him.

Forgive us our trespasses.

We entered the door into the chapel from the courtyard and were led immediately down the stairs, rather than inside. Our guide, Nabil, paused before we made our way down, pointing out a Plexiglas-covered hole in the stone that opened up to a small room below. This, he said, is where we believe they dropped Jesus down into that chamber. We know this because the early Christians marked it, with crosses that can be seen around its perimeter. My heart dropped as I imagined the Son of God being tossed down a chute as if he were waste, or dirty laundry, landing on that cold and dusty floor with a thud. I imagined the early Christians sneaking in with sharp objects, leaning over to scrape away stone in a desperate attempt to remember what had happened and where, as if to honor him by their solemn recollection. This was such a bittersweet contrast to the statue outside, this evidence of Christians who steadily carved these crosses so faithfully. They knew him, the crosses whispered, and they remembered what was done to him. They would always remember.

The chambers below, used as prison cells, were appropriately cold and unnerving. I did not want to take the time to pray; I wanted to leave quickly. I could not stop thinking about a crumpled Jesus on the floor, and a denying Peter outside, and a scattered band of disciples God knows where, and a cross mere hours away. I prayed with short breath, staring at the hole above, etched in remembrance: forgive us our trespasses.

I was ready to leave after we clambered back up the steps. The roosters were not comical any longer; they were true. And the truth of them felt exhausting.

I did go into the chapel, though, and then above, to the sanctuary. I braced myself for more evidence of our human disloyalty and fickle virtue. I took a deep breath and walked in.

There was evidence of our fickleness and disloyalty everywhere. There were more mosaics of Peter denying Jesus, of Jesus being arrested. But there were also mosaics of Peter confessing his love for Jesus on the shores of Galilee, of Peter as the first pope, of

Jesus and the disciples at the Last Supper. The church told the truth about Peter's worst mistake, but it did not leave the rest of Peter's story untold. And it did not leave the rest of Jesus's story untold, either. A cross-shaped window spans the vast expanse of the domed ceiling, a radiant array of color and light with the risen Jesus at its center. Circling the edges of the dome, golden-robed angels dance, hands stretching both up and out. Color was bursting everywhere: blue and green walls, orange ceiling, gold arches, warm jewel tones in icons.

The Church of St. Peter in Gallicantu is an appropriately sobering place, but it is also a place of deep grace that bursts forth in a spectrum of resplendent color. In this church, we all stand in the face of our own unrighteousness. That's the point, actually: God made him who had no sin so that we might become *his* righteousness. Ours, as it turns out, is not particularly trustworthy.

As I prayed in the sanctuary, I tried to hold in my heart all of the events housed in this place: the denial, the arrest, the imprisonment. All of them are denials of one kind or another, some in word, others in action. How often we deny the person of Jesus, as if we can snuff him out or minimize his life. But we don't understand Jesus if we think we can do that. If we think we can do that, *non novimus illum*. We don't know him at all.

Forgive us our trespasses, Lord. And we know, they are great. They are often unspeakable. But somehow, you have returned our stumbling for your grace and you have clothed us in your righteousness. We are shocked to be glowing in the radiance of your love. You have made even a place of error into a house of worship. You have reminded us, convinced us, of the most important truth we can know: we are loved. Not because we are perfect, but because we are yours.

And so, it seems, a church dedicated to a colossal mistake may not be that odd of an idea after all. Maybe the best place to hear we are forgiven is in one that remembers how badly we can mess up. Maybe the strangest thing about Christians is that we have the audacity to remember with a church building how big a mistake all of us can make, do make, will make. Maybe that's strange only on the outside of grace. Because when you walk inside the doors of grace, you realize you can face your mistakes because you've been forgiven, because you're loved in spite of them.

There is a church in Jerusalem that is named after one person's worst mistake. Only a people doused in grace would do such a thing. We have asked for God to forgive our trespasses, and God has answered yes. We are forgiven, and that gives us the freedom to live as God's holy people, after even our worst day. Let the cock crow. Perch him on the dome, front and center. We are forgiven.

● ● ● ● ● ● ● ● ● ● ●

Our Father, who art in heaven, hallowed be thy name;
Thy kingdom come, thy will be done on earth as it is in heaven.
Give us this day our daily bread, and forgive us our trespasses,
as we forgive those who trespass against us.
And lead us not into temptation, but deliver us from evil,
For thine is the kingdom, and the power, and the glory,
forever and ever,
Amen.

16

Via Dolorosa

Jerusalem

●　●　●　●　●　●　●　●　●　●

Pilgrims have been walking the Via Dolorosa, the Way of Sorrows, since the mid-fourth century. This is a journey that follows the footsteps of Jesus from when he was condemned to death by Pontius Pilate to his crucifixion at Golgotha and his burial. The path itself has changed over the years, as have the stops or stations. Originally, walking the Way of the Cross was a practice begun in Europe for those Christians who could not make the journey to Jerusalem and yet wanted to remember the Passion. Churches and monasteries began to set out small shrines and altars outside of their edifices, so that as travelers went from town to town, they could stop along the way. In Jerusalem, the practice of Byzantine pilgrims was to walk the Way without stopping. The route changed in the eighth century, beginning instead at the Garden of Gethsemane and moving through Mount Zion before coming into the city. In the Middle Ages, two routes emerged, with Western Christians veering on a westerly path and Eastern Christians heading east. In the fourteenth century, Pope Clement VI appointed the Franciscans to guide and instruct pilgrims on the

Via, and this led to the development of eight stations, walked in reverse order, beginning at the Church of the Holy Sepulchre and ending at Antonia Fortress.

By the eighteenth century, the fourteen stations we now know had been decided upon, mostly because they had become standard practice in Europe and the desire for congruence influenced Jerusalem to do the same. The path itself, however, returned to being close to the original path designed by the Byzantine Christians.

Historically speaking, the Via Dolorosa does not necessarily match the exact locations of Jesus's path. Early Christians believed a fort called the Antonia Fortress, built by Herod the Great and named for Mark Antony, marked the place where Jesus was condemned, scourged, and forced to take up the cross. Excavations in the nineteenth century revealed ancient pavement that seemed to match the cobblestone used at the time of Jesus, which was designed to prevent horses from slipping. It has since been determined that the pavement postdates the time of Jesus, but the flooring does provide a glimpse into what streets would have been like.

The route today begins just inside the Lion's Gate in the Muslim Quarter and ends at the Church of the Holy Sepulchre in the Christian Quarter, stretching a third of a mile. Nine of the stations can be found along the bustling streets of the Jerusalem Cardo, while the final five lie within the Church of the Holy Sepulchre. Each of the stations is marked with a plaque, but they can be difficult to locate without a guide. Many pilgrims choose to walk the Via Dolorosa with the Franciscans, who do so every Friday at 3:00 PM, which is thought to be about the time the historical events happened. Of course, the streets are flooded on Good Friday each year with Christians from all over the world who have come to remember the events of the Passion during Holy Week. (There is a description of each of the fourteen stations in the appendix.)

Then the soldiers led him into the courtyard of the palace (that is, the governor's headquarters); and they called together the whole cohort. And they clothed him in a purple cloak; and after twisting some thorns into a crown, they put it on him. And they began saluting him, "Hail, King of the Jews!" They struck his head with a reed, spat upon him, and knelt down in homage to him. After mocking him, they stripped him of the purple cloak and put his own clothes on him. Then they led him out to crucify him.

MARK 15:16–20

For thine is the power.

The Via Dolorosa was not at all like I had imagined. I had been told that its path wove through the bustling Jerusalem Cardo. I had been told the path was hard to follow, and easy to lose. I had been told it would be disorienting. And still, I was not prepared.

I think this is how the disciples must have felt. All of those times Jesus told them, tried to warn them, tried to give them an idea of what was to come. . . . His words may as well have fallen on deaf ears. No matter what the disciples had possibly anticipated, in every case imaginable, they would have been wrong. They would not have been ready for this, would not have seen this coming. Nobody was prepared. Nobody is prepared still, and we have been pondering it for two thousand years.

Nobody expects God to die.

Even now, when you try to speak the truth of that day out loud, people are eager to hush you, to rush you straight toward Easter as if all the other things never happened, as if they were all a dream, a nightmare not to be spoken. Jesus died. And nobody was expecting that.

Who could have imagined a crown of thorns for the King of kings? Who could have envisioned a purple robe made for mocking? Who would have conceived of a cross so heavy to bear that the Son of God would need help carrying it up a hill toward his own death?

Who would have thought that all the disciples would scatter?

The Via Dolorosa begins at a relatively quiet section near the Lion's Gate. We walk on, pausing inside a chapel that remembers Jesus being beaten and scorned. I try to pray the Lord's Prayer. I hardly finish. We move out into the street again, with this word *power* stuck in my throat like a burgeoning cry. *For thine is the power.* How can that be? How is that true here? I see no power, no glory, and no forever: only mockery, and condemnation, and forever's opposite, death.

We continue on. Our guide, Nabil, maneuvers us through the street, to the left, around the corner. He is pointing out plaques and church facades. We are crowded and shoved by passersby on their rush to whatever is next. We are surrounded by pastry booths and fake pashmina scarves and knockoff handbags and dozens of tchotchkes made in China and wooden incense burners and roasting peanuts and NBA sports hats and glittering bracelets and plastic sandals and cheap T-shirts displaying flags and curse words and SpongeBob SquarePants. I am trying to keep my focus, to hold on to some semblance of a center, but I cannot fathom the depths of Christ's pain while standing next to all. of. this. stuff.

The whole path feels like a sort of gruesome hide-and-seek game, looking this way and that for pieces of a puzzle nobody wants to see completed.

At the eighth station, a Greek monastery features a cross inscribed on the wall. Surrounding it are the Greek letters IC XC NI KA, meaning "Jesus Christ is victorious." Each duet of letters resides at one of the cross's intersections—top left, top right, bottom left, bottom right. Jesus Christ is victorious. What does that mean, here in the middle of the Cardo, when his journey to the cross is not yet finished? What does it mean to be victorious in the midst of all of this chaos, all of this noise?

The Via Dolorosa, the Way of Sorrows, is a statement of power. It is a statement of what power does when it is corrupt, evil, broken, angry, afraid. It is a statement of what power can do when it is wielded as a weapon, as a silencing force, as a threat. The stations speak of the power of the Roman Empire. They can condemn Jesus, beat Jesus, direct Jesus, force Jesus. They can push their power onto Jesus until he bleeds, falls down, and collapses under the weight of their might.

The cross is a symbol of humiliation. It is a way of lifting up someone in order to make a mockery of them, a spectacle of them. It is a way of enforcing an empire's power over life itself. They have had enough of this instigator Jesus. They have had enough of his healings and teachings and crowds. He will no longer stand defiantly against the political rule of Caesar and the social rule of his empire. They will use all the power at their disposal. They will silence him.

Jesus, the one others claim to be the Son of God, the king of the Jews, the Messiah, indeed stands silent before Pilate. He does not raise a defense. He does not protest the verdict of the empire. He does not refuse his cross. But we must not think for one second that he does not stand in his power. The cross of Christ is the very power of God, the very glory of the Son of God. Jesus saves us by showing us what the power of God looks like, and it looks like faithfulness even unto death upon a cross.

We had been told the path was hard to follow, and easy to lose. We had been told it would be disorienting. And still, we were not prepared. We could never be prepared, not for this, not for this harrowing way of sorrows. We do not have the power to stand firm in the midst of the chaos that is the very death of God.

But Jesus does.

Jesus did. And because of that power, this story ends not on a hill but in a garden.

At the intersection of power stands the cross. Indeed, the cross stands *as* the intersection of power, the ultimate collision of mercy and violence. Jesus is resolute, even as he is stretched left and right and up and down. He does not give in. He does not let go—not of his humanity, not of his divinity, not of us. He stands in his power, which is his love poured out for every last one of us. His is the only lasting power there was, is or ever will be.

Nobody expects God to die. But then God went and did the most surprising thing of all: God turned the powers of the world upside down, so that even death upon a cross could become eternal life.

●　●　●　●　●　●　●　●　●　●　●

Our Father, who art in heaven, hallowed be thy name;
Thy kingdom come, thy will be done on earth as it is in heaven.
Give us this day our daily bread, and forgive us our trespasses,
as we forgive those who trespass against us.
And lead us not into temptation, but deliver us from evil,
For thine is the kingdom, and the power, and the glory,
forever and ever,
Amen.

17

The Church of the Holy Sepulchre
Jerusalem

●　●　●　●　●　●　●　●　●　●

The Church of the Holy Sepulchre is a labyrinthine building that bears the marks of its multiple power struggles and iterations. Christian tradition has definitively claimed this area as the site of both the crucifixion and the tomb. The church is located in what is now the heart of the city, though in the time of Jesus this area would have been located outside the city walls. Originally an abandoned quarry, this area contained one or more raised rocks that would have been an ideal platform for Roman executions. In addition, less than fifty yards away was located a collection of tombs, one of which is said to have belonged to Joseph of Arimathea.

The Church itself was built during the time of Constantine, after the demolition of a pagan temple. Constantine's church was laid out like a rectangle stretching from east to west. The entrance, which faced the Cardo, opened into a narthex that led into the main church, at whose southwest corner resided the rock of Golgotha. The church then continued into an open courtyard that led to a large dome over the presumed tomb of Joseph of Arimathea. Other kokhim, or tombs, fanned out in an arc around it.

The church was decimated in 1009 and has yet to be restored to its original layout. As it now stands, visitors enter what would have been the open courtyard. Straight ahead one finds the Stone of Anointing, a nineteenth-century addition, which remembers Jesus's being anointed for burial and also reminds pilgrims of the story of Mary Magdalene anointing Jesus's feet. To the right is the rock of Golgotha, where a long line awaits pilgrims as they take turns putting their hand on the glass-paneled stone that is said to have held the cross. To the left is a nineteenth-century wooden aedicule (small shrine) inside which lies the tomb. The line for this is also perpetually long.

The Church of the Holy Sepulchre is maintained by four branches of Christianity: Eastern Orthodox, Roman Catholic, Armenian, and Ethiopian/Coptic. (The roof of the Church of the Holy Sepulchre is maintained by Ethiopian monks and is the site of the Crypt of St. Helena. Though it is on the current roof, this would have been street level to Constantine's church.) Over the years, these branches have not always shared easily or well. After multiple skirmishes that even served as a contributing factor to the Crimean War of 1854, a treaty was reached called the Status Quo, specifying the privileges each group holds here. To ensure cooperation, a Muslim family in Jerusalem was given the key to the church as well as the responsibilities of opening and closing it each day. A descendant of this same family continues this duty to this day.

Then they brought Jesus to the place called Golgotha (which means the place of a skull). And they offered him wine mixed with myrrh; but he did not take it. And they crucified him, and divided his clothes among them, casting lots to decide what each should take. It was nine o'clock in the morning when they crucified him. The inscription of the charge against him read, "The King of the Jews." And with him they crucified two bandits, one on his right and one on his left.

MARK 15:22–27

Forgive us.

A range of human emotions is on display inside the Church of the Holy Sepulchre. Hundreds of pilgrims head this way and that, bustling past others without a thought, some with heads down, many with heads and camera phones tilted up. Some stand in the center of busy walkways, clustered together and forming makeshift traffic barriers. In a sense, you could be anywhere, and this is what you would see: people, with their own agendas, living with little thought to the needs of others.

On the other hand, almost anywhere you look within the large compound of the church, people are displaying deep signs of faith and devotion. An elderly woman, head down, arms outstretched, rosary in hand, cries at the Stone of Anointing. Next to her, a study in generational contrast, a young girl, head bent, sets her rosary and smartphone on the stone in prayer, as if for blessing. In the line to the site of Golgotha, people begin to fidget—or grow very still—as it nears their turn to kneel, and to place their hand upon the stone. Some do it quickly, some more slowly; others pause, and wipe their eyes as they leave. As one moves from there to the aedicule to see the empty tomb, the energy changes, from deep and moody to frenetic. The line is less somber, more bustling and eager. People light candles along the outside of the aedicule as they wait, often with obvious emotion.

This is to say nothing of the rather disjointed religious symbolism of so many Christian sects displayed here and there: Orthodox chandeliers and icons, Catholic crosses, Armenian tapestries. It is as if all of Christian history is equally stuffed into this place, like a house without enough storage. Cluttered, crowded, and incohesive, but in its own way, beautiful.

A range of human emotions, from fear to solemnity to passion and devotion to frenetic joy: it's likely one will feel all of these things while at the Church of the Holy Sepulchre. The Cross and the Resurrection, these are events that quite literally fill the range of human experience, from the lowest depths of hell to the highest praise of heaven. They are all here, and it is as if one can almost feel the weight of that fullness, that range, even while walking around.

All this can be overwhelming. It can be difficult to find a place to ponder, to think clearly, to take notice. At first, I found this frustrating, waiting in line for the site of Golgotha, attempting to clear my mind and ready my heart and be present. But of course, this is exactly the experience of Golgotha itself. Every step from the Via Dolorosa to the Church of the Holy Sepulchre was a flawed and difficult attempt to find centeredness and peace in the midst of chaos. It was not just the inner chaos that comes from remembering this event; it was the chaos of remembering, or perhaps realizing for the first time, that this event happened in the midst of daily life, while street vendors still went to work that morning and stayed all afternoon, while stonemasons and seamstresses did what they did the day before and what they would do the day following. To walk the Via Dolorosa, the stations of the cross, to this church is to be reminded rather blatantly that life went on that day for so many, while the life of the One who would change the world was coming to an end.

As I knelt down to set my hand upon the stone of Golgotha, I closed my eyes and tried not to drown out the sound of the surroundings but to bring them into the Lord's Prayer. The most fitting thing, the most honoring and sacred, seemed to be to let this place be exactly what it was and nothing else: cluttered, crowded, beautifully and tragically incohesive. Here was the range of human experience, brought to the very cross of the One whose human experience would transform us all, deliver us all, forgive us all.

Forgive us our trespasses: these words in this space seemed to hold worlds within them, as if the depths of the universe could be found there. Forgive us, God. We are an absolute mess. Even in this place, especially in this place, we have no idea how to honor you, make sense of our lives, share freely with one another, or walk humbly with You, our God. We cannot even manage the keys to this place of worship, warring children that we are. Suddenly, Jesus's prayer to God for unity becomes poignant; whatever we all are, we are not one. We are cordial neighbors, perhaps. We are polite acquaintances. We are strained relatives. But we are not one. Forgive us our endless trespasses, Lord. We are all still scattered like sheep without a shepherd. We are all still cluttered and confused and incohesive.

What do we do when One so holy, so beautiful, so filled with mercy and justice and love and grace comes to show us the way to live? We crucify him. Lord have mercy, we crucify him, while half the city goes on as if nothing is even happening.

All of this felt heavy, to be sure, but the strangest part—the part that makes little worldly sense but perhaps perfect gospel sense—is that rather than feeling shameful, guilt-laden, or depressed, I had a palpable feeling all around of gratefulness. Belovedness. Yes, forgiveness.

Whatever the worst of humanity could throw at Jesus, he did not let us change him. He did not falter, stumble, or sway. He remained resolutely our Savior, forgiving the criminals on his left and his right, forgiving the crowds throwing stones and insults, forgiving every last one of us until all that is left is his life of love, come to redeem all of us from our lives of brokenness and confusion.

One cannot walk from the stone of Golgotha to the aedicule of the empty tomb without realizing that all is forgiven. He is not here; he is risen. He has risen above our own penchant toward violence, our bent toward destruction, even our fear of the holy. He has risen above it all so that love has come fully, so that forgiveness can be felt to the depths of our bones. Forgive us, we pray, and in Jesus, we hear a resounding Yes, again and again and again.

● ● ● ● ● ● ● ● ● ● ●

Our Father, who art in heaven, hallowed be thy name;
Thy kingdom come, thy will be done on earth as it is in heaven.
Give us this day our daily bread, and forgive us our trespasses,
as we forgive those who trespass against us.
And lead us not into temptation, but deliver us from evil,
For thine is the kingdom, and the power, and the glory,
forever and ever,
Amen.

18

The Church of St. Anne

Bethesda/Jerusalem

● ● ● ● ● ● ● ● ● ● ●

There are a number of things that make the Church of St. Anne unique. For one, much of its current structure is original. The church was constructed and expanded between 1131 and 1138 using traditional Romanesque architecture, which includes multiple pillars and high arches, and cross-vaulted domed ceilings. The interior manages to look simple and impressive at the same time. The structure lends itself to near-perfect acoustics, and it has become a favorite singing place for pilgrims and choirs and soloists from around the world. Amazingly, rather than being destroyed in 1187, the Church was converted into a madrasa, and by the fifteenth century it was the most respected school in all the city. This kept it not only intact but in good condition for over five hundred years.

In a strange turn of events, the church was gifted to the French by the Turkish Ottoman Sultan Abdulmecid I, who gave it to Napoleon III in thanks for French support in the Crimean War of 1856. The madrasa had long since been abandoned at that point, and it was quickly falling into disrepair. The church has since been owned by the French government, and the White

Fathers, a Catholic order known for their white robes, continue to serve as its keepers.

It began as a Byzantine basilica, named after Anna and Joachim, parents to Mary the mother of Jesus, who was said to have been born here. The church was built at what was believed to be the birth site of Mary, and pilgrims can descend the south steps to find the grotto as well as an altar to Mary.

It was also built over two of Bethesda's pools, and, remarkably, one of the Byzantine piers remains intact today. To make matters more confusing, there is actually another Byzantine-turned-Crusader church just next to the Church of St. Anne. It was built on the remains of what used to be a pagan shrine to the Greek god of healing, Asclepius, which is the reason why people in Jesus's time flocked to the pools of Bethesda for healing. One of these pools remains today, accessible by a steep staircase from the ruins above. There is still water in it.

Now in Jerusalem by the Sheep Gate there is a pool, called in Hebrew Beth-zatha, which has five porticoes. In these lay many invalids—blind, lame, and paralyzed. One man was there who had been ill for thirty-eight years. When Jesus saw him lying there and knew that he had been there a long time, he said to him, "Do you want to be made well?" The sick man answered him, "Sir, I have no one to put me into the pool when the water is stirred up; and while I am making my way,

someone else steps down ahead of me." Jesus said to
him, "Stand up, take your mat and walk." At once the
man was made well, and he took up his mat and began
to walk.

JOHN 5:2–9

Deliver us.

In all my life, I never would have guessed that any of the pools of
Bethesda still had water. But they absolutely do. It's murky water,
in which you don't particularly want to dip your head, or your toe.
But going down those steps toward the ancient pool, in what is
now the deep underground, covered with dirt and grass and a few
layers of ruins—the waters there are waiting for you.

The Lord's Prayer started singing itself in my mind as I descended the steps, like a summoned song my heart knew I needed before
my head could ask for it. Perhaps it was because at that moment,
on that day, I had traveled already from the Mount of Olives to
the Church of the Holy Sepulchre, experiencing the heaviness
that inevitably comes from walking those hard roads with Jesus.
Bethesda was a healing place. It was a sanctuary, a moment to take
a breath and feel, just for a moment, like you could be back in
Galilee. It was refreshing, like pools of water ought to be.

It doesn't hurt that Bethesda is also a serene respite from what
can be a very loud and crowded Jerusalem. It seems miles from
all the hustle and bustle of the Cardo, even though it's only about
fifty yards away. The ruins in and of themselves are compelling,
their high arches and stone steps painting a vivid picture of
what could have been in years long before. And it's green—lush,

velvety, carpeted green—as one would expect from a place near natural pools.

A plaque overlooking the ruins informed readers the pools were a shrine to Asclepius, which adds another important texture to the story of the man who was healed here by Jesus. Asclepius, the Greek god of medicine and healing, had a robust cult following, and temples dedicated to him sprouted up across the Roman world. These temples were most often located on hills outside of towns (which is true for Bethesda) and near springs or wells that were believed to have healing powers. Pilgrims would travel to the temples in search of healing, including the man we read about in John 5. There he sat, day after day, trying to make his way to the waters when they were ritually stirred. Nobody ever noticed him. If they did, they didn't help. From what the man said, it sounds like the most common response was to push him out of the way. And then here comes Jesus, with one simple question: Do you want to be made well?

Jesus did not ask whether the man believed in him or not. He did not ask the man to renounce Asclepius. He did not ask whether the illness was the man's fault, or why the man hadn't figured out how to get down to the water after all this time. He asked the one question that mattered, the question that lay at the heart of it all: do you want to be made well?

Do you want to be healed? Are you content the way you are, even if you're suffering, or do you long for change? Are you willing to experience change? No matter how you got here, no matter what you've done, no matter what others have done to you: do you want to be well?

Leaning toward those now-murky waters, I could feel my answer thrumming in my chest. Yes, I want to be healed. And not only of any infirmities, and certainly not as one who has suffered as that man had suffered. But more importantly, as one who has too often been guilty of passing others by, rendering them invisible, pushing them out of the way in my quest to get where I'm going. I want to be healed of asking less important questions, of passing judgment rather than lending a helping hand. Do we want to be made well, whole, new?

Yes. Deliver me.

These pools where people came day after day, vulnerably exposing and announcing their need for healing to the world, they are the waters of deliverance. And deliverance is healing, of course. They are one and the same. The waters of restoration, of wholeness, flow over us and we are reborn, remade, redeemed.

The Church of St. Anne, which sits adjacent to the pools and the ruins, is pleasantly asymmetrical, in a way that echoes its quirky history as a church that changed not only hands but also religions through the years. Columns on one side do not echo the column adjacent, and windows are not of a uniform size. From the outside, it looks more like a fortress, really, than a church, but it remains in shockingly pristine condition. What an odd turn of events that kept this church intact when most all the others had fallen; what serendipity, that even when it had been abandoned, it found its way even through a handful of wars until it came round again to the safekeeping of the Christians. The name Bethesda means "house of mercy," and it seems Bethesda's church has born the name well. It, too, is a place of deliverance: delivered from intended destruction and disrepair, birthed once again into a place of worship and song for pilgrims across the world.

As I made my way into the church and into a pew, again this phrase "deliver us" resounded as I prayed. Through the waters of baptism and the pools of healing and the storms of the Sea of Galilee we come to the One who is our Deliverance. We are born again, awash in mercy, enveloped in love. We want to be well and so we are made well, in but a moment. Deliverance feels less heavy here, more festive. It feels full, like deliverance is not only deliverance *from* illness, but also deliverance *to* wholeness. In the sanctuary, it felt something like special delivery, like a package unexpected but longed for all the same, like something you wanted so badly but almost dared not to hope for, lest it not come true. Deliver us, we pray, deep in the recesses of our hearts like a childlike whisper on Christmas morning.

Our guide, Nabil, insisted we sing in the sanctuary. He told us that choirs come here from all over the world to benefit from this little quirky church's acoustics, and we would be remiss not to experience it ourselves. When we lifted our voices in song, it was as if Andrea Bocelli had taken over our voices and sent them into the rafters. I have never sounded so good in all my life. This felt, to me, like a special delivery, like we were joining the chorus of heaven. Perhaps indeed, we were. The song of deliverance rings true here. It resounds, clear as a bell.

This church has survived in its pristine condition only because it has been cared for and nurtured by Christians and Muslims, in turn, and multiple nations, too: Israel, Turkey, France. It has been passed from one hand to the next for nearly nine hundred years in a relatively peaceful fashion, something that should be expected but is sadly unique. Its walls and arches and floors resound possibly because they have been held together by something larger than brick or mortar. Rather than being torn apart, this place has been kept whole. Maybe that's why you feel more whole when you visit here. Perhaps that's why our songs seem to echo heaven as they rise to the rafters here: they are part of the biggest, most beautiful song of all, the Song that knits us all closer together and makes us one. Harmony is our ultimate deliverance, from all that seeks to separate us from each other and from the God who made us all. That is the chorus of heaven, the joy of harmony: multiple voices, sounding unique unto themselves and yet coming together to voice the Truest thing.

Do we want to be well? Yes, we do. Deliver us, Lord. Bring us a special delivery, that we may delight in you and in the life you have given us.

Here we are, ready to pick up our mats and walk again.

● ● ● ● ● ● ● ● ● ● ●

Our Father, who art in heaven, hallowed be thy name;
Thy kingdom come, thy will be done on earth as it is in heaven.
Give us this day our daily bread, and forgive us our trespasses,
as we forgive those who trespass against us.
And lead us not into temptation, but deliver us from evil,
For thine is the kingdom, and the power, and the glory,
forever and ever,
Amen.

19

The Church of the Nativity

Bethlehem

●   ●   ●   ●   ●   ●   ●   ●   ●   ●

The Church of the Nativity is more specifically the combined site of two churches and a crypt, as well as numerous small chapels. Similarly to the Church of the Holy Sepulchre, the Church of the Nativity suffers the wounds of many years of interdenominational and interfaith battles. Consequently, the interior can prove confusing, as multiple Christian groups manage different sections. However, it is able to lay claim as the longest continually operating church in the entire world.

The church was built in AD 339 by Constantine and dedicated to his mother Helena. It was destroyed in the mid-sixth century in a revolt, after which it was rebuilt by Emperor Justinian I. Persian invaders planned to ransack the church in 614, but after seeing the wall mosaics of the Wise Men, who resembled Persian priests, it was spared. It was then restored during the Crusader period. The church currently is in need of great repair, particularly of the roof, which has never recovered from an earthquake in 1837. The restoration process has gone slowly, as the many Christian sects have had difficulty agreeing on a number of decisions.

Adjoining the Church of the Nativity is the Church of St. Catherine, a Roman Catholic church designed in the Gothic revival style. This is where Christmas Eve midnight Mass is celebrated with great festivity each year. In addition, there is a Chapel of St. Joseph to remember the angel's appearing to Joseph, a Chapel of the Holy Innocents to remember those children who were killed by Herod's decree, and a Chapel of St. Jerome, to commemorate the place where Jerome completed the Latin Vulgate translation of the Bible.

Pilgrims usually enter on the Greek Orthodox side, whose doorway is remarkably low. This is a mark of the Mamluk period, where the doorway was fixed so as to prevent horses from entering. Beyond the entrance there is a set of trapdoors on the left that reveal the remains of the original fourth-century floor. Toward the south are stairs leading to the Cave of the Nativity, with its fourteen-point star that marks the place of Jesus's birth, and nearby, a space that marks the place where Jesus slept in the manger.

In those days a decree went out from Emperor Augustus that all the world should be registered. This was the first registration and was taken while Quirinius was governor of Syria. All went to their own towns to be registered. Joseph also went from the town of Nazareth in Galilee to Judea, to the city of David called Bethlehem, because he was descended from the house and family of David. He went to be

registered with Mary, to whom he was engaged and
who was expecting a child. While they were there, the
time came for her to deliver her child. And she gave
birth to her firstborn son and wrapped him in bands
of cloth, and laid him in a manger, because there was
no place for them in the inn.

LUKE 2:1–7

For thine is the kingdom.

Authority rests upon his shoulders. That's the first thing that came
to my mind while kneeling in the small nook where it is said Mary
laid Jesus to sleep in the manger. "For a child has been born for
us, a son given to us; authority rests upon his shoulders, and he
is named Wonderful Counselor, Mighty God, Everlasting Father,
Prince of Peace" (Isaiah 9:6). All that hope, beauty, potentiality—
all lying there in a manger in a sleeping baby. We Christians are
strange indeed, to proclaim that the world will be upturned and
amended by a child king.

Of all the places we acknowledge power and authority, none is
so shocking and odd as on the tiny shoulders of a baby. What kind
of kingdom is this, that its future begins in such a vulnerable place
as a nursery located in an out-of-the-way cave?

Of course, kings are not new to this city. Bethlehem is, after all,
the City of David. And yet, as surprising a choice as David was to
become king despite his many older brothers, there is little com-
parison to the surprising presence of God that comes to us through
a young girl whose child was foretold by an angel. Any child king
seems rather preposterous; a divine King, a God-made-human
child king, is nothing short of absurd. What kind of king, much

less the Son of God, is born in such a quiet way, such a hushed fashion, such a mundane and humble beginning?

There is a funny door at the Greek Orthodox entrance to the church, the primary entrance used by pilgrims. It was reduced in size to a mere four feet high and two feet wide when there was a fear that soldiers on horses might come charging in, or that looters might bring in carts and abscond with the church's treasures. Centuries later, it still remains as is, most likely because it's so difficult for the varying Christian groups to decide together on anything at all. I can't help finding it apropos, this act of squatting down as you enter into the place of Jesus's birth. It reminds me of a story I once heard of a student who asked a rabbi, "In the olden days there were people who saw the face of God. Why don't they anymore?" The rabbi replied, "Because nowadays no one can stoop that low."

We may have to bend low to walk through the Door of Humility, as the entrance is affectionately called, but that's nothing compared to the unpretentiousness of God's being born as a poor child in a rural town of nobodies. When we prostrate ourselves to God, we are merely mimicking what God has done for us.

I made my way down the crowded steps toward the grotto below, waiting in a long line of diverse pilgrims eager to remember the birth of their Christ. When my turn came, I knelt first at the star, placing my hand where Jesus is said to have been born. And then I made my way just to the left and behind it, down a few small steps, again bending low, kneeling down at the place of the manger. It isn't easy to find the space and quiet to pray the Lord's Prayer in the busy traffic of the Cave of the Nativity, but if you tuck your head under the manger and close your eyes you can find a sacred moment to pause, pray, and ponder what it means that the coming kingdom of God began as a newborn child.

The Church of the Nativity exposes all the ways we cannot seem to figure out how to live into this peaceable kingdom, choosing instead to fight over authority and control even in the place meant to honor the One who overturned them. God help us, we have worshiped the Prince of Peace in one breath and drawn swords in the next. What would it mean for us to return to the essence of this place, to the simplicity of this manger, to the radical notion that God has chosen to become God-with-us and has done so not with fanfare but with a small and faithful family of little means. And with a baby. One sleeping baby, here on this manger hearth. For his is the kingdom.

I am grateful and dazzled by this thought; at the same time, I can feel myself terrified for him, even now. Imagine him sleeping there, Mary and Joseph nearby, all unaware that soon enough the kingdoms of this world will start coming for him, starting first with Herod and ending with the full power of the Roman Empire itself. In between, he will bring discomfort to every kind of power this world has to offer: political and economic power, religious power, powers of class and gender and ethnicity, powers of nation and state. He will even disrupt natural powers—disease, storms, a simple loaf of bread. This child is King, and there is no place on which his authority does not rest.

He will replace all those misplaced attempts at power with the only force that can undo them: the unconditional, unwavering, unfaltering love of God. When this Prince of Peace is finished, there will be no place—and no person—on which the authority of his love will not rest.

At Advent, we celebrate a season of light, which is a way of reminding ourselves that love has come into the world and is always coming into the world and will someday fill up this world until it overflows in new creation. We celebrate a season of swords being beaten into plowshares, and of lions becoming vegetarians, broken people becoming whole people, and of signs that will ask everything of us. The prophet Isaiah speaks of a time when those who have walked in darkness will see light, a time when we will have our burdens removed from our shoulders and our joy increased, a time when the marching boots and the blood-stained coats of warriors will be tossed into a bonfire to be used no more.

In a word, we will all be disarmed.[2] Oppressors will be disarmed from their positions of power, the oppressed will be disarmed from their positions of defense, the politics-wielding peacekeepers will be disarmed from their words of compromise and their weak treaties. The yokes will be broken and so will the governing rods. The marching boots of nation against nation will be tossed in the fire, useless, because no one will take to the streets for such a reason any longer. We will be disarmed, not by tanks or armies, but by a baby. For his is the kingdom. Authority rests on his shoulders, not upon the shoulders of a dictator or a revolutionary. It rests upon his shoulders, and there it will remain.

In the midst of a world of strife and aggression, we find ourselves face-to-face with this inconspicuous child. We find ourselves completely disarmed—emotionally, mentally, rationally, *literally*. We drop our weapons and take up shovels because we just can't imagine doing anything else after seeing the face of this child.

Jesus came in the fullness of time, which meant good things were on the horizon but which also meant very disturbing and jarring things were underway. Jesus came in the darkness, the chaos, in the vulnerable body of a teenage girl, because the love of God is nothing if not the power of God opening up to the deepest shadows

---

2. This word came to me thanks to a sermon by Jürgen Moltmann entitled "The Disarming Child" in his book *The Power of the Powerless* (New York: Harper and Row, 1983).

of human experience, which include powerlessness and dependence on other's hands. If we are to be people of God's kingdom, we do so by realizing first that God has radically placed himself in our hands in the form of a newborn child. God's kingdom begins with an astonishing redefinition of authority that includes not only a fully human God but also two fully human, imperfect, temporal parents who must protect him from all that seeks to harm him in the days ahead.

For now, crouched in the manger of the Nativity in the grotto of this old basement, eyes closed, I rejoice that authority rests upon his newborn shoulders. I pray. *For thine is the kingdom.*

Quiet, inconspicuous, crowned only with hay, clothed only with human skin and swaddling clothes, armed only with love. Blessed be this child, Emmanuel. His is the kingdom, indeed.

●　●　●　●　●　●　●　●　●　●　●

Our Father, who art in heaven, hallowed be thy name;
Thy kingdom come, thy will be done on earth as it is in heaven.
Give us this day our daily bread, and forgive us our trespasses,
as we forgive those who trespass against us.
And lead us not into temptation, but deliver us from evil,
For thine is the kingdom, and the power, and the glory,
forever and ever,
Amen.

20

Shepherds' Field

Bethlehem

●　●　●　●　●　●　●　●　●　●

In the town of Beit Sahour on the eastern side of Bethlehem is the area known as Shepherd's Field. From here, one can see an overview of Bethlehem, including the Church of the Nativity, and to the east, the Herodium, where King Herod built a bunker into the side of a hill that is also assumed to be the place of his tomb.

There are two places of worship where pilgrims have gathered in Shepherds' Field to recall the nativity story. The first, and perhaps the most likely, is the Greek Orthodox church known as Kanisat Al-Ruat (Church of the Shepherds). It is built on the site of a fourth-century church mentioned by a number of ancient sources (Eusebius, Egeria, and Arculf) as the place the early Christians celebrated. It is also believed to be the site of the Tower of the Flock, where Jacob traveled as he grazed his sheep after his wife Rachel passed away. Though a new sanctuary stands there now, adorned with a distinctive red-tiled roof, the remains of the fifth-century church remain intact; in fact, it is the most preserved church of its time outside of Jerusalem.

A quarter mile to the north, one will find the Chapel of the Angels, a Roman Catholic site owned and maintained by the Franciscans. The sanctuary, which adjoins the remains of yet another fourth-century church and monastery, was built in 1954 and is meant to resemble Bedouin tents; the only light comes in through skylights that pepper the domed ceiling. Bright and beautifully detailed paintings adorn five domed apses, and the white walls are embellished with golden lettering declaring, "Gloria in excelsis Deo" (Glory to God in the highest).

Just a few feet from the sanctuary is a natural cave that has been partially enclosed, giving pilgrims a sense of the shepherds' traveling accommodations. Star-shaped skylights have been carved into the soot-blackened roof so that even inside one can recall the starry night sky.

In that region there were shepherds living in the fields, keeping watch over their flock by night. Then an angel of the Lord stood before them, and the glory of the Lord shone around them, and they were terrified. But the angel said to them, "Do not be afraid; for see—I am bringing you good news of great joy for all the people: to you is born this day in the city of David a Savior, who is the Messiah, the Lord. This will be a sign for you: you will find a child wrapped in bands of cloth and lying in a manger." And suddenly there was with the angel a multitude of the heavenly host, praising God and saying,

"Glory to God in the highest heaven,
and on earth peace among those whom he favors!"
LUKE 2:8–14

Glory.

The Chapel at Shepherds' Field may very well have been the most joyful sanctuary I visited in the Holy Land. Its stunning domed ceiling beckons your eye skyward even as the murals on the surrounding walls envelop you in warm, richly saturated colors. Even the white walls and arches convey lavishness rather than sparsity, their tone full, communicative, and enlivening. As I traversed the perimeter to take in the details of each painting, I laughed as I saw dogs accompanying the shepherds and their herds. They were fitting additions, even if they were not historically definitive participants. They made the sanctuary feel even more like "home," and when we're celebrating God's making a home among us, that feels felicitous.

As I began to pray, ambulating, eyes open to take in all the lush details and bright vivacity of the place, the Lord's Prayer came bursting out of my heart and into my mind in the form of song. I sang it to the tune of "Angels We Have Heard on High," which did not necessarily fit perfectly in word form, but could not have fit the moment more absolutely. Gloria!

Gloria in excelsis Deo! I sang in my mind, my heart lifting like a kite. I felt transported back to my childhood, and I could hear my choir teacher's voice as she reminded us to enunciate as we sang "egg-shell-seas" with a clap, clap, clap of rhythmic fervor. "Can you hear it?" she'd ask us. "In/egg/shell/sees/Daaaay-O!" as she clapped her hands at each syllable and stomped around the room in her black closed-toed heels. And we could. We could all feel it, when we sang it like that, attuned to each other and lifted up into the pull of the song, like a parallel dimension: joy.

We were all, regardless of age, children of joy in that moment. Mouths puckered into perfect little O's, eyes ablaze with life and light, chests raised high and lungs full. Gloria. Glorious.

I could not have been more delighted when our group of pastor-pilgrims started singing Christmas carols in the cave nearby. We puckered our mouths into O's as we rode the notes up and down like a twisting slide of song, our hands above our heads to enjoy the ride and feel the wind at our fingertips and in our hair: Glooooooooooooooooria! Our voices bounced off the cavernous walls, sooty ceiling, and musty floors. I sang with reckless abandon, because that's what your heart does in a place like this. You remember what you were made for: praise, and joy, and a heart that delights in the glories of this world and its Maker, Savior, and Keeper. You were made to be loved and to discover that love with boundless, overflowing joy. You were made to see stars, to witness miracles, to watch love be born into the world, to proclaim it ever new each morning. You were made to be delighted by this one, simple, mind-blowing fact, over and over again: God has made God's home among us, right in the middle of our Everyday Fields.

Glory.

We often make this such a heavy word—such a serious word, as if it is to be carried around in intricately adorned and mightily padlocked treasure chests, filled with something so rich but such a burden to carry. As if it's been sitting locked at the bottom of the sea, and we have to do some smuggling to get into it. As if it's always blinding in a bad kind of way, in an eclipsing kind of way that will age us as it did Moses when he came down Mount Moriah, white-haired and fear-stricken for seeing something he felt unready to behold. This is how the shepherds felt about it, anyway.

They were terrified, the NRSV translation says, though I'm fonder of the phrase the King James Version uses: they were sore afraid. How else do you feel when something as big, explosive, and all encompassing as God's Gloria shines all around you? You feel sore afraid, like you want to duck into that cave until the glory passes, a more benevolent angel passing over your door.

But sometimes God's Gloria comes in the most perfect packages: small and crinkly, smelling of what we can only call heaven. Sometimes God's Gloria doesn't age us, but it makes us children again and again.

The Glory of God is good news of great joy for all the people, because it is the most needed news in all the world: God has come to live with us. Love has come here, and it has come to stay.

Joy abounds in these Fields of the Shepherds. So, then, let the glory of the Lord shine around us, and let us not be afraid.

May we be like children, puckering our mouths into O's of praise, lifting our hearts with reckless abandon, skipping and jumping and dancing as we watch this Love unfurl around us. Love has come, and He. Is. Glorious.

● ● ● ● ● ● ● ● ● ● ●

Our Father, who art in heaven, hallowed be thy name;
Thy kingdom come, thy will be done on earth as it is in heaven.
Give us this day our daily bread, and forgive us our trespasses,
as we forgive those who trespass against us.
And lead us not into temptation, but deliver us from evil,
For thine is the kingdom, and the power, and the glory,
forever and ever,
Amen.

ACKNOWLEDGMENTS

First and foremost, I am forever grateful to the Cousins Foundation for providing me with the extraordinary opportunity to travel to the Holy Land and to join such a meaningful cohort of local pastors. Your generosity is beyond measure, and the pilgrimage was, for me, a fountain of blessing overflowing. And much thanks to the Macedonian Ministry Program, for all you did for me and for so many other pastors to ensure a seamless, wonderfully executed trip. The church is brighter because you've inspired so many of her pastors through your benevolence and care.

To Jon Sweeney and everyone at Paraclete Press: thank you for giving this book wings. This book is, for me, a love letter, and it was with great trepidation that I searched for a publishing home I could entrust with its contents. Thank you for being so trustworthy. And to Phyllis Tickle, whose idea it was to send the book there: I always take your advice, and I'm always grateful I did.

To my fantastic cohort of fellow pastor-pilgrims, to whom this book is dedicated: I am so grateful for the memories, and the laughs, and the uproarious theological discussions at the table and on the bus and walking along the streets of Jerusalem. We traveled to Jerusalem as colleagues, but I do believe we returned as dear friends. To Nabil: believe me, I'm telling you, you're the best. And to Thaer, thank you for being our fearless, candy-dispensing, perpetually smiling driver.

And, of course, much love and thanks to my dear family, Dan, Mia, and Grant, for affording me not only two weeks away from our busy and wonderful life, but also many hours behind a closed office door pounding out these words of remembrance. I love you all to the moon and back.

Even after writing a book about my pilgrimage, I am not sure I will ever be able to put into words what I experienced there. Or, to be more precise, Who I experienced there, and how. It is a daunting thing to attempt to put words to the sacred. I know I did so feebly, or, as St. Paul would say, through a glass, darkly. My hope is that despite the smallness of these words, you would, by the power of God's Spirit, enter into the holy ground that is the ever-presence of God. God is with us, always. This is perhaps the most important truth that was anchored into my soul those fourteen days. May you know that to be true, wherever you are, and may God's presence bring us all peace and grace, and, in due time, the fullness and wholeness of new life.

A Brief Guide to the Via Dolorosa Stations of the Cross

Jerusalem

Begin at the Lion's Gate in the Muslim Quarter of the Old City. Walk forward past St. Anne's Church.

STATION 1

Jesus is condemned to death (Mark 15:7–14). The location of what is thought to be the Antonia Fortress is not accessible, as it is on the property of the Al-Omariya elementary school. Look for the plaque on the left wall across from the Monastery of Flagellation.

STATION 2

Jesus is scourged and takes up his cross (Mark 15:20–21). Find the Franciscan Chapel of Flagellation and Chapel of Condemnation, with the plaque on the same side before you reach the Ecce Homo arch and the Sisters of Zion Convent. Take note inside the church of the three intricate stained-glass windows depicting Pilate washing his hands, Jesus being scourged and crowned with thorns, and Barabbas being released.

STATION 3

Jesus falls under the cross the first time. Continue walking forward until you reach El-Wad Street. Turn left (southeast), and you will see a relief sculpture of Jesus falling under the cross above the door of the Polish church. The words "Station III" are fashioned into the wrought-iron gate underneath as well.

STATION 4
Mary encounters Jesus. Just ahead and also on your left is the Armenian Church of Our Lady of the Spasm.

STATION 5
Simon of Cyrene takes up the cross (Mark 15:21). On the corner where El-Wad meets Via Dolorosa Street, on the right, there are words etched in a large white stone doorway as the road narrows and moves uphill.

STATION 6
Veronica wipes Jesus's face with her veil. Continue up Via Dolorosa Street on the left, further west up the hill, where you will find the Chapel of Saint Veronica, sometimes called the Church of the Holy Face. Look for the station plaque inscription on a stone pillar between the two blue doors of the church.

STATION 7
Jesus falls a second time. Two interconnected chapels at the intersection of Via Dolorosa and Souk Khan El-Zeit mark this station.

STATION 8
Jesus consoles the women of Jerusalem (Luke 23:27–31). Keep straight ahead and cross the market street and go up the steps to Saint Charlambos, a Greek monastery. Inscribed on the wall is a cross and, surrounding it, the Greek letters IC XC NI KA, meaning "Jesus Christ is victorious."

STATION 9

Jesus falls a third time. Turn around and head back toward Souk Khan El-Zeit, turning right to take you to the "back door" of the Church of the Holy Sepulchre. Walk up the twenty-eight steps to reach the Coptic church, located on the roof. A Roman column built into the church door is the location of the ninth station.

STATION 10

Jesus is stripped of his garments. Proceed down the steps and backtrack, turning right onto Souk Al-Dabbagha. The final four stations are located at the Church of the Holy Sepulchre, whose entrance will be readily visible a few yards down on the right. Station 10 is in the Chapel of the Divestiture. At the entrance on the right, you will see white stone steps leading up to an arched window.

STATION 11

Jesus is nailed to the cross. Remain inside the church, where you will see the mosaics in the Roman Catholic chapel (also called the Latin Calvary) that mark this station.

STATION 12

Jesus is crucified (Mark 15:22–24). The Greek Orthodox Calvary contains the Rock of Golgotha, a silver circular plate marking the cross. It is situated underneath an altar and is usually accompanied by a line of visitors; each person has a turn to kneel down and peer under the altar.

STATION 13

Mary anoints Jesus's body for burial (Luke 23:55–56). The Stone of Unction, now located at the entrance of the church, is made visible by the many pilgrims who kneel and pray at it, placing rosaries and other relics atop it for blessing.

STATION 14

Jesus is placed in the tomb (Mark 15:42–47). Circle around to the left side of the church, where the aedicule on the main floor reveals the location of Jesus's tomb. Though it seems disorienting to notice the close proximity of Golgotha and the garden, archaeologists have indeed confirmed that the aedicule is located in what was a first-century "cemetery." Perhaps it is for this reason that Joseph of Arimathea offered his nearby tomb to the crucified Christ.

SELECTED BIBLIOGRAPHY

Levine, Lee I. *Caesarea under Roman Rule*. Leiden: Brill, 1975.

Metzger, Bruce M., and Michael David Coogan. *The Oxford Companion to the Bible*. New York: Oxford University Press, 1993.

Miller, J. Maxwell. *A Pilgrim's Guide to the Holy Land*. N.p.: Macedonian Ministries, 2010.

Murphy-O'Connor, Jerome. *The Holy Land: An Oxford Archaeological Guide: From Earliest Times to 1700*. Oxford: Oxford University Press, 1998.

Walker, P. W. L. *In the Steps of Jesus: An Illustrated Guide to the Places of the Holy Land*. Grand Rapids, MI: Zondervan, 2007.

• • •

If you would like to learn more about the architecture of many of the churches in the Holy Land, there are a number of online and print resources available. Architect Antonio Bertuzzi is responsible for a good number of the churches in the Holy Land.

ABOUT PARACLETE PRESS

WHO WE ARE

Paraclete Press is a publisher of books, recordings, and DVDs on Christian spirituality. Our publishing represents a full expression of Christian belief and practice—from Catholic to Evangelical, from Protestant to Orthodox.

We are the publishing arm of the Community of Jesus, an ecumenical monastic community in the Benedictine tradition. As such, we are uniquely positioned in the marketplace without connection to a large corporation and with informal relationships to many branches and denominations of faith.

WHAT WE ARE DOING

Paraclete Press Books

Paraclete publishes books that show the richness and depth of what it means to be Christian. Although Benedictine spirituality is at the heart of all that we do, we publish books that reflect the Christian experience across many cultures, time periods, and houses of worship. We publish books that nourish the vibrant life of the church and its people.

We have several different series, including the best-selling Paraclete Essentials and Paraclete Giants series of classic texts in contemporary English; Voices from the Monastery—men and women monastics writing about living a spiritual life today; award-winning poetry; best-selling gift books for children on the occasions of baptism and first communion; and the Active Prayer Series that brings creativity and liveliness to any life of prayer.

Mount Tabor Books

Paraclete's newest series, Mount Tabor Books, focuses on liturgical worship, art and art history, ecumenism, and the first millennium church, and was created in conjunction with the Mount Tabor Ecumenical Centre for Art and Spirituality in Barga, Italy.

Paraclete Recordings

From Gregorian chant to contemporary American choral works, our recordings celebrate the best of sacred choral music composed through the centuries that create a space for heaven and earth to intersect. Paraclete Recordings is the record label representing the internationally acclaimed choir Gloriæ Dei Cantores, praised for their "rapt and fathomless spiritual intensity" by *American Record Guide;* the Gloriæ Dei Cantores Schola, specializing in the study and performance of Gregorian chant; and the other instrumental artists of the Gloriæ Dei Artes Foundation.

Paraclete Press is also privileged to be the exclusive North American distributor of the recordings of the Monastic Choir of St. Peter's Abbey in Solesmes, France, long considered to be a leading authority on Gregorian chant.

Paraclete Video Productions

Our DVDs offer spiritual help, healing, and biblical guidance for a broad range of life issues including grief and loss, marriage, forgiveness, facing death, bullying, addictions, Alzheimer's, and spiritual formation.

Learn more about us at our website: www.paracletepress.com or phone us toll-free at 1.800.451.5006

SCAN TO READ MORE

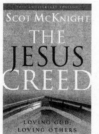